THE IMPACT BLUEPRINT

Make an Impact Today!

Joe Schmidt

THE IMPACT
BLUEPRINT

A STEP-BY-STEP
JOURNEY TO A LIFE
OF **SIGNIFICANCE**

JOE
SCHMIT

ISBN 13: 978-1-63489-196-7

Library of Congress Catalog Number: 2018967090

First Printing: 2019
23   22   21   20   19   5   4   3   2   1

Cover and interior design by James Monroe Design, LLC.

Wise Ink, Inc.
807 Broadway St. NE, Suite 46
Minneapolis, MN 55413

www.wiseink.com
To order, visit www.itascabooks.com or call 1-800-901-3480.
Reseller discounts available.

To my Dad, Elmer Joseph Schmit.
You left us in 1984, but in many ways,
I have spent every day since then
trying to make you proud of me.

CONTENTS

Introduction | 1

THE IMPACT BLUEPRINT

INTRODUCTION

Roy Griak was the longtime head coach for the University of Minnesota men's track and field and cross-country teams. He led young men for thirty-three years after being an assistant coach for almost twenty years. Roy bled the school's colors, maroon and gold.

In his Hall of Fame career, Coach Roy's teams won three Big Ten titles and finished fourth in the NCAA cross-country finals, which is very difficult to do for a school that has snow on the ground five months out of the year! He coached forty-seven cross-country and track and field All-American athletes, including three NCAA champions, sixty Big Ten individual champions, and several Olympians.

Roy died on July 9, 2015, at the age of ninety-one. There is probably not a coach, professor, or administrator in the history of the University of Minnesota who made a bigger impact than Roy Griak. That is a big, bold, bodacious statement to write about one person, but you would have a hard time finding anyone associated with the university who would disagree.

Another Hall of Fame coach at the University of Minnesota saw Roy Griak nearly every day for thirty-three years. Gary Wilson was the head coach of the women's track and field and cross-country teams at the University of Minnesota during the same time frame. Gary said Roy treated everyone the same, whether they were the king of Sweden or homeless. "His magic was that he cared about people as human beings, and because of that, he got the most out of his athletes." Gary went on to share that until Roy died, he hand-wrote Christmas cards to every athlete he ever coached.

When it became public news that Roy was dying, I read many tributes to him posted on social media and other outlets. I recognized the names of many who were sending their love, respect, and emotional tributes. Some were successful athletes, but there were many trainers, secretaries, and opposing coaches too.

The more I read, the more two things became very apparent. One, I started to feel a tremendous amount of guilt. As the sports director at KSTP-TV in Minne-apolis and St. Paul, I covered Gopher sports and could only remember doing two interviews with Roy over the previous thirty years. Like every other news outlet, we spent most of our time at the university covering football and basketball, the so-called "revenue sports."

The second important revelation I had was startling and powerful. Not one of the tributes I read said anything about Roy's ability to coach and improve an athlete's performance. No one said they could never have been a Big Ten champion without their Coach Roy. No one thanked him for helping them get to the Olympics. The postings all said things such as, "I am a better person because you came into my life," "I just closed the biggest business deal of my life using Roy Griak 101," and "I am a better spouse, parent, and friend from the lessons you taught me." When it was all said and done, the championships and trophies didn't mean as much as the impact Roy made on people's lives. Roy Griak lived a life of significance because he knew how to make an impact.

In my first book, *Silent Impact,* I tell stories of people who truly understand that it's the larger collection of things they say or don't say and the things they do or don't do that all work together to make a lasting impact. They care, and they make meaningful connections. It becomes part of their DNA, and they figure out that it's not about other people liking them; it's about them feeling good about themselves.

Each chapter in this book is designed to enlighten and inspire you to make an impact on your world. You may choose to read it in one sitting, or you may choose to read one chapter a week, in which case you'll stretch it out over the course of a year! Each chapter ends with an Impact Resolution, a specific thing to think about, focus on, or do in the upcoming week to strengthen that particular trait. Our research has shown that people who live a life of significance are more aware and more intentional with the impact they have on others. It is a part of their DNA. This is an opportunity for you to ramp up your impact game.

> *Each chapter in this book is designed to enlighten and inspire you to make an impact on your world.*

We would all like to live a life of significance, and this book will give you the daily and weekly focus you need to make a difference. You will be happier and more productive, and you'll enjoy deeper friendships than ever before.

I have a few suggestions on how we can keep the weekly Impact Resolutions at the top of our minds:

- Write the word of the week on a sticky note and place it on your bathroom mirror.

- Put the trait in a visible place on your phone or computer.

- At your work space, have a special notebook or file where you can respond to the prompts each week. Use it to brainstorm things you want to talk about with a trusted friend. Come up with your own ideas on how to make your Impact Resolution part of your genetic code.

1

INTROSPECTION

When I do workshop sessions with companies, I often conclude one of my talks with a photo of Mount Rushmore. I give everyone in the room an opportunity to build their own monument, honoring the four people who have had the biggest impact on their lives. I often challenge them not to name their parents for this exercise. This exercise always turns out to be a powerful experience for everyone.

The easiest way to live a life of significance is to emulate the people on your personal Mount Rushmore. What did they do to help your career, make you a better friend or parent, give you the wake-up call that you needed, or help you through a hardship?

I usually ask participants to share their Mount Rushmore selections with the people at their table. It's a great team-building exercise because it tends to be an unintimidating way to get to know people on a deeper level. There's much more empathy and kindness to go around if colleagues understand each other's stories and what makes them tick.

One of the most difficult and unpredictable careers has to be working in the corrections field. I especially felt this way after giving a keynote and breakout session to the Minnesota Department of Corrections. The audience consisted of leaders from various correctional institutions in Minnesota. Many of these managers deal with guards and staff who have been assaulted by inmates. In 2017, there were hundreds of incidents reported in Minnesota prisons. These highly trained law enforcement officers eat stress for breakfast. I assure you, this is a group of tough men and women.

When we did the Mount Rushmore exercise, I was surprised at how open and personal this group got when we started discussing who was on their list and why. Then Marc Magnuson told his story. It was so powerful that the room was mesmerized. He said that his brother Tim was on his personal monument, but he would not have even considered including him on that list until a few years ago. Tim lived in Columbus, Ohio, but because of his northern Minnesota upbringing, he grew up a huge hockey fan. When Columbus was awarded an NHL franchise in 2000, he wanted to get a job with the franchise just to be a part of the team. He started as an usher and eventually became the elevator attendant who served the media, players, coaches, and their families.

In December of 2016, Tim was diagnosed with ALS—Lou Gehrig's disease. He worked as long as he was physically able, and the franchise did everything they could to keep him involved. Even when Tim was no longer able to do his job, he was invited to the locker room to say hello to the guys before games. He had no idea that he had become an inspiration to this tough, hard-nosed hockey team. Every member on that team knew Tim was the toughest guy in the locker room.

In a local television interview, John Tortorella, the head coach of the Blue Jackets, got emotional when he talked about Tim and the impact he had on his young hockey team. "It's hard to see a guy care so much about the team and have so many things go on. We love the guy."

Before the playoffs started that season, the team had a coin designed to remind them of their goals and what they should focus on as they prepared for their quest to the Stanley Cup. Tim's initials were on that coin and on the sleeves of the team's warm-up gear. Tim had nicknames for almost every player, and nobody left a conversation with him without feeling better about themselves. Keep in mind, this was for a man who pushed buttons on an elevator.

When Tim lost his battle with ALS in September 2017, almost the entire team showed up at his funeral. Machismo meant nothing that day, as many could not hold back tears. Tim's brother, Marc, said it was like the scene in the movie *Remember the Titans* where the players all walked past the casket for one last goodbye.

Tim's ability to make connections and care about others made him a person of impact. "He really made people feel at home. He liked people and remembered everyone's name," Marc said. He also shared a little-known fact about Tim. It turns out that he was quite an athlete when he was young. He was recruited and was on the track and field team at the University of Minnesota for one year. And his coach was Roy Griak. Does this make you believe in the ripple effect of impact?

IMPACT
RESOLUTION

Make your own Mount Rushmore of Influence. Think of people who changed you, the way you work, or how you live. Maybe they gave you great advice, or maybe they gave you a kick in the rear just when you needed it. Think hard because your Mount Rushmore is a monumental decision!

2

HAPPINESS

If you get a degree from the prestigious Yale University, you can pretty much write your own ticket. It's difficult to get into, even for superior students! You'll never guess the most popular course in the history of this famous Ivy League school. It is called "Psychology and the Good Life," and it helps students differentiate between things that will truly satisfy and things that will bring only superficial or temporary happiness. This class on happiness is so popular that over one thousand students try to get into the class each semester!

We live in a world filled with stress and pressure, resulting in more mental-health cases than we have ever seen before. That is why this course at Yale is so popular, and that's why we all need to be challenged to look at our lives to see if we are doing everything we can to be truly happy.

Dr. Laurie Santos is the instructor for this popular course. She told the *New York Times* that some students see Psyc 157 as an easy class, but she says it's actually the hardest class at Yale. To see real change, students need to be willing to work on themselves. This is hard for high-achieving students who have found much success already in their young lives. Their final is what Dr. Santos calls a "Hack Yo'Self Project," which requires planning and launching a personal self-improvement mission.

Think of the happiest person you know. Just the thought of this person likely brought a smile to your face. I always get a kick out of going to Disney World, which is famously known as "the happiest place on earth." When the kids and their parents rush into the park in the morning, you can just feel the joy and anticipation. But around three o'clock, when the children and most parents need a nap, you will see the kids and their parents lose it. It is no longer the happiest place on earth.

I know a man who has found and studied the happiest people on earth—and, no, his name is not Walt Disney. I'm referring to Dan Buettner, a National Geographic Fellow and bestselling author of *The Blue Zones of Happiness*. He has been examining what makes human beings happy and healthy for the last fifteen years. At the World Economic Forum's annual meeting in 2018, he shared his extraordinary findings on what drives happiness in individuals and how it varies in different countries. He made his presentation in front of world leaders, Nobel Prize winners, and industry titans.

"If you want to be happier, change your environment, not your behavior," Buettner told me. It's impossible to measure happiness, but you can measure life satisfaction, and for that to happen, he says three things must come together: pride, pleasure, and purpose. Money does not bring you happiness, but it does help you meet your basic needs. Health is important to happiness. As a matter of fact, the happiest people in the world live an average of eight years longer, according to research described in *The Blue Zones*. Buettner also says to do your best to sleep at least seven and a half hours a night. He reports that people who sleep six hours a night are 30 percent less happy than people who sleep more.

When I asked Buettner what he changed in his personal life after traveling the world researching happiness, he said, "I have a very clear vision of what my purpose is." He says he works an average of six to seven hours a day. He gets eight hours of sleep no matter what his circumstances. Additionally, he committed to eating plenty of vegetables and purged some friends from his inner circle who were just too negative.

Buettner shared a couple more tips on being as happy as possible. He says to limit time on social media to no more than an hour a day. For some people, this is way out of control! He also says that statistically, people who have a pet are happier, as are people who live near water.

With people battling depression and anxiety in alarming numbers these days, happiness has never been more important. It's a choice, it takes some intentionality, and it might not actually be solved by a trip to see Mickey Mouse and Friends!

IMPACT
RESOLUTION

This week, write down three things that really make you happy. Make sure they fall into the categories of pride, pleasure, and purpose. Then make them your priority and be prepared to relish in the happiness that follows.

3

JUDGMENT

There are only a few people in this world who have permission to pass judgment on others. If you happen to sit on a bench wearing a black robe and others refer to you as "Your Honor," then you are one of those people. Judge Chris Wilton had been on the bench in Scott County in Minnesota just a little over a year when a twenty-two-year-old, heroin-addicted, eight-months-pregnant woman stood before him with a probation violation. Jennifer faced a year in jail, and that would have been an automatic ruling for many judges.

"She had a sparkle in her eye. I saw a fighter and thought she had a chance," Judge Wilton said. When

Jennifer entered the courtroom, she was high. She did not apologize for it but did admit she was concerned about her baby. Judge Wilton took that as a sign of hope. He put her in jail for a week and made sure that she got the medical care she and her unborn baby needed.

Jennifer was released from jail and soon gave birth to a baby boy who had to suffer through heroin withdrawal. Judge Wilton required her to appear in his courtroom every three weeks, not only to see how she was doing but to offer her encouragement. "I would give her something to do every time she appeared, like get her driver's license or something else pretty small. I would then encourage her, tell her how great she was and how proud I was of her."

Even though Judge Wilton gave her structure and support, Jennifer failed two more drug tests. He put her in jail five weekends in a row. "I made her kiss her baby and sent her to jail." He said that Jennifer had an attitude, but because of the baby, she had dreams and did not lose hope. Neither did he.

After no less than twenty-seven appearances in Judge Wilton's courtroom, Jennifer was released from probation. She had been clean for 444 days! Then Jennifer did something that caught her judge completely off guard. She asked if he would be willing to officiate her wedding in a few months. Jennifer said she really believed Judge Wilton's faith in her was the reason she was alive and thriving today.

A relatively new judge showed enormous wisdom and compassion in this case. He went the extra mile and helped Jennifer turn her life around. When asked about it, Judge Wilton admitted that there were colleagues around the county who disagreed with his approach.

The impact Jennifer's case had on how Scott County works with drug offenders has been remarkable. It is now called "Treatment Court," which is more positive-sounding than "Drug Court." Even though it's impossible to save everyone, the instincts of one judge led the county to understand that many other drug addicts are also looking for help.

Judge Wilton told me of another offender he worked with who was middle-aged and had been an addict for years. He was able to get clean, and Judge Wilton asked him what he was most looking forward to. The man said he was excited about spending Christmas with his family because jail, being high, or running from the police had kept him from home for the past seven holidays.

People of impact like Judge Wilton are not looking for headlines or pats on the back. However, the story got out and even appeared on a national broadcast of *CBS News*. Judge Wilton was "shocked that people cared so much." As we ended our conversation, I asked him to describe his ultimate lesson learned. His answer was simple and powerful. "You can't give up on people."

On October 7, 2017, Judge Chris Wilton officiated Jennifer's wedding to her husband, Bill. He admitted it was very emotional. "To see her in a wedding dress, smiling, clean of drugs, and happy was nothing short of a miracle." The couple is expecting their second child this year. Their firstborn, Jaxson, is a normal, energetic little boy with two parents who love him very much.

Jennifer said, "I never could picture a happy family, but I found a good guy who saw something in me." She also said that at first, she thought Judge Wilton was mean to her, but she soon realized that he made her feel like she could do it.

IMPACT
RESOLUTION

This was a story about a judge being less judg-mental. That's the lesson we should all take away from this story. The next time you make a judgment about someone before you know their story or consider their great potential, remember this story about Jennifer and Judge Wilton. Consider someone in your life who feels judged. Go out of your way to encourage that person this week.

4

COURAGE

Dan Stock and Bob Truax owned a gym in Roseville, Minnesota, for serious weight lifters. They noticed that the gym clothes on the market were not made for the serious weight lifter. Sweatpants in particular were boring, did not fit well, and certainly did not match the image of their iron-pumping clients. Dan and Bob saw a problem and went to work to solve it.

They invented a pair of sweatpants that were baggy, had a comfortable elastic waistband, and had a colorful pattern. They were called Zubaz! Either you or your parents had a pair of them. Their first classic design was a zebra pattern, and they got wilder from there. Before they knew it, Dan and Bob had a fast-growing company. In 1991 alone, the company did 100 million dollars in business. Their slogan was "Dare to be different." It worked because these guys had the courage to go for it. And in turn, people had the courage to wear Zubaz in public!

Another courageous risk-taker was Steve Jobs of Apple. In his famous 2005 Stanford commencement speech, he said, "Have the courage to follow your heart and your intuition. They somehow know what you truly want to become."

In *The Wizard of Oz*, the Cowardly Lion was looking for courage, and when he finally found it, he realized it was just a state of mind. There is physical courage that we all admire, but moral courage is what we are talking about today. When you look at people who changed the world throughout history, the one trait they all had in common was courage. Martin Luther King, Gandhi, Mother Teresa, Nelson Mandela, Rosa Parks, Winston Churchill, Helen Keller, and on and on. Behind their courage was a moral conviction that fueled their efforts.

IMPACT
RESOLUTION

This week, look back at your life and remember a time that you showed great courage. Then look back at a moment you wish you could have displayed more courage. Don't beat yourself up because of it, just let yourself imagine what would have happened if you could have been a little braver. Next time, you will find the courage that will push you to dare to be different!

5

INITIATIVE

There's an old joke about a boss who asks his employee, "When are you ever going to take some initiative?" And the employee responds, "As soon as you tell me to." We all know people like that, don't we? We also know people who have the ability to get the job done without looking for a pat on the back. They have a spark of energy and motivation that spurs them to take initiative.

Robert Kennedy once said, "Some men see things as they are and ask why. I dream of things that never were and ask why not." He said that in the late 1960s, and I am sure if he said it today, he would include women like Cary Weatherby. Cary left her career as a construction coordinator for building developers to become a stay-at-home mom. If there is one thing we all can agree on, it is to never underestimate the power of a mom who takes initiative.

As a volunteer in her children's schools, Cary noticed that many teachers took money out of their own pockets to pay for items needed in their classrooms and sometimes for supplies needed for their students. Cary also noticed that many companies were getting rid of things that teachers could use, such as paper, pencils, desks, chairs, and even filing cabinets.

At the intersection of her three passions—helping kids, recycling and reusing, and making an impact—Cary started a nonprofit organization called Companies to Classrooms, where she worked as the executive director for twelve years. The organization served nine school districts in the Twin Cities area. Reusable office materials were kept out of landfills and placed in classrooms to benefit teachers and students, where they will stay for years to come.

Companies to Classrooms maintained an eight-thousand-square-foot warehouse, which was filled to the brim with supplies that registered teachers could access monthly to help with the needs in their classrooms. Companies such as Cargill, Dairy Queen, General Mills, and Medtronic loved to donate to the organization because it gave them an outlet for their waste.

One of the best job interview questions ever asked is, "Could you give me an example of a time where you showed initiative?" In every average interview, the candidate will say they are a hard worker and a self-starter. If they struggle to answer this question, of course the search for a new employee should continue. Always be honest in answering that question. Taking initiative is not the easy way, but it's a sure way to make an impact.

Taking initiative is not the easy way, but it's a sure way to make an impact.

IMPACT
RESOLUTION

What have you been putting off for a long time? This week, take the initiative to tell someone about it and find a way to get it started. Where there is motivation, there will be progress. The satisfaction that comes from seeing something that needs to be done and doing it will be yours!

6

ACCOUNTABILITY

If I have one pet peeve from working in the TV news business, it is that when a mistake is made, people spend too much time trying to figure out who to blame instead of figuring out how to keep from making the mistake again in the future. The blame game is almost never productive. It can help hold someone accountable, but not before there is a lot of damage. Whether we are the parent, the boss, or the teacher, we all have two choices. We can find and blame the culprit, or we can put our time and energy into solving the problem and preventing future problems.

When we conducted some internal research to find what makes the best coworkers, we found that people value those who are accountable, not only to themselves but also to the team. These valued colleagues want to get the job or project done and are not looking for a pat on the back. Their satisfaction comes from within.

In my career as a sportscaster, I have encountered hundreds of coaches with different coaching styles and philosophies. That means I've covered everything from the tough ones who use fear as a motivation to the so-called "player's coaches" who want to be liked by all the players. Yellers, screamers, motivators, teachers, and those who showed kind love, tough love, and no love—I have seen them all. No matter what their style is, the coaches who have the most success are the coaches who preach, teach, and demand accountability. They let the athletes know what their role on the team is and exactly what is expected of them. With these types of coaches, there is never any question of where you stand with the coach or with the team.

> *No matter what their style is, the coaches who have the most success are the coaches who preach, teach, and demand accountability.*

Tony Dungy and Brian Billick were both regular guests on a thirty-minute sports show I hosted every Sunday night during the years they were both assistant coaches for the Minnesota Vikings. They both went on to become head coaches in the NFL and both led their teams to Super Bowl victories, Coach Dungy with the Indianapolis Colts and Coach Billick with the Baltimore Ravens. Their styles could not be any more different! Coach Dungy was quiet, measured, and unemotional, but he was very demanding. Coach Billick was innovative, emotional, and considered by many to be arrogant. Despite their different styles, both of these coaches led their teams to the Vince Lombardi Trophy because they were accountability wizards. They communicated expectations and got results. Under their leadership, everyone did their part.

In our personal and professional lives, we must be accountable for the things we can control. This includes our attitude, our energy, our commitment, and ultimately our success or failure. Accountability is accepting our responsibilities and being willing to take action on them.

I believe that accountability partners, whenever possible, are a great idea. Whether it's for working out, breaking a swearing habit, or adopting a new Impact

Resolution each week while reading this book, an accountability partner will help keep you on track. I've found, in my seminars and keynote speeches on company culture, that relationships work best when accountability is built in.

What do you want your personal or professional life to look like, and how can you hold yourself accountable to guidelines that will help you reach your goals? Too many times, people worry about letting someone else down. After all, our standards for ourselves are generally higher than any standards others might place on us.

As leaders, how do you hold your team accountable? This question is applicable to most professional environments and is worth considering. In sales, the old adage is that a confused mind never buys. A confused employee never buys into the company culture, goals, or processes for accountability. On the other hand, high-performance teams know exactly what is expected of them, and they are given the tools they need to accomplish their tasks.

IMPACT
RESOLUTION

This week, make the commitment to find an accountability partner who will help you raise your game, and in turn, be willing to do the same for them or for someone else. Generally, those who invite accountability are high achievers who stay focused and reach their goals. With an accountability partner, you'll take it to the next level!

7

LIKABILITY

My friend Phil has a big personality. When he meets a mutual friend or someone he knows he's going to hit it off with, he extends his arm for a handshake and says, "Hi, my name is Phil Sibinski. How do you like me so far?" It may be the best icebreaker ever; it's impossible not to like Phil. He sells quality products, but he sells more than most because he is Likable.

You don't have to look too far to find successful people who are not very Likable. Steve Jobs was a genius, but nobody ever described him as high on the Likability chart. But here is a fact that is undeniable. Everyone likes to be liked. If you have a Facebook account, admit it: you check to see how many likes you got on each beautiful picture or well-crafted post. The people who are most Likable tend to be genuine, friendly, and interested in the person they are speaking with at that moment.

I once called on Bill Popp, the owner of POPP Communications, to see if he would be interested in being the major sponsor of a charity golf tournament that I was working on for Big Brothers Big Sisters of the Greater Twin Cities. As a sportscaster, I knew Bill was a limited partner of the Minnesota Timberwolves, but I didn't know him well. He agreed to help out and remained a major sponsor of our event for the next sixteen years!

Like a lot of these events, we had a silent auction to raise more money for this great mentoring organization. Someone donated an autographed edition of Hank Aaron's new autobiography, *I Had a Hammer*. He was one of my sports heroes growing up, and I wished I could own that signed book, but my wife and I were just starting our family and did not have a lot of extra cash to spend, even for a charity. I tried, but every time I placed a bid on the book, someone outbid me. It got up to over $100, and I decided to just go to the bookstore and buy it without the autograph. After the dinner and awards ceremony were over, our committee was busy cleaning up when one of the volunteers came to me with something in hand and said that someone wanted me to have it. It was the autographed Hank Aaron book. Bill Popp, our major sponsor and my new friend, kept bidding it up to see how far I would go. He knew all along he was going to give it to me regardless!

The second year of the tourney, one of the volunteers pointed out that Bill Popp was helping to pick up all the garbage along with the other volunteers. It did not surprise me. Bill became the most Likable guy to our entire volunteer team; he knew all their names. What a guy!

In TV, consultants get paid to uncover a news, sports, or weather anchor's Q rating. This is qualitative research to find out how highly regarded that person is in the industry. In other words, how Likable are they? Think of your favorite TV anchor. I bet you like them even though you might not know them personally.

We are not all TV personalities, but we do all have our own brand. What is your personal brand? Are you Likable? Let people know you care, hand out generous compliments, smile often, and be authentic. There is no question that the more Likable you are, the more positive an impact you will make.

IMPACT RESOLUTION

This week, figure out two or three things you can do to be more Likable without forcing it. It might be as simple as handing out compliments or making a call to someone you have not connected with in a while. Be authentic, be Likable, and make an impact.

8

FORGIVENESS

Somebody once told me the most powerful two-word sentence ever written is "Jesus wept." It is hard to argue with that, but I think I know the second most powerful two-word sentence: "I'm sorry."

You are going to have a hard time finding one trait in this book that has more impact than forgiveness. It's also one of the hardest to master because it's not easy. You have two choices when someone does you wrong. You can get bitter or you can get better. I am always shocked when I see victims of crimes forgive the perpetrators. They show far more intestinal fortitude than I think I could muster.

My high school has a class reunion every five years, and I try to make every one of them. As I was driving to my most recent reunion, I kept thinking about one of my classmates who I had never seen attend a reunion. I will call her Rebecca.

Rebecca was different, and because of that, she got picked on. I wasn't the instigator, but I certainly wasn't innocent. I would laugh at the mean comments, throw a few wisecracks in myself, and not have the guts to stop the nonsense that was going on. Today we would call it bullying. Back then it was being mean and just not right. Many years later, I was embarrassed about both my actions and also my lack of action.

When I arrived at the reunion, one of the first people I saw was Rebecca, and I knew what I had to do. Later in the night, I asked Rebecca if we could talk. She looked at me with surprise but agreed. After asking her some questions about her life and her family, I came right out and said I needed to apologize. I told her I was sorry for everything that happened all those years ago.

She told me that this was the first class reunion she had attended and that she had actually turned the car around two times on the way to the event. She finally thought, *The heck with it. I am strong, and I am going to the reunion.* We both shed a few tears and Rebecca accepted my apology. That was a great moment, but it wasn't the best moment. When the night ended, she came up to me, gave me a big hug, and said that she would see me in five years. That was the best moment.

Since that time, we have become friends and keep in touch through social media. Here's what I learned about forgiveness. It really felt good to have Rebecca forgive me. It allowed me to forgive myself. When I speak to high school students, I tell this story and challenge them not to be that mean girl or that macho guy who thinks he or she is better than everyone else. I challenge them to speak up when someone is being bullied or mistreated. If I can reach a few kids, it is worth opening up.

At one of the pre-wedding parties before my wife, Laura, and I got married, people were asked to write down a few words of advice for the young, stunning couple. (We are not young anymore, but my wife is still stunning.) My father-in-law, Roger Sahr, wrote words I never forgot. His advice was, "This too shall pass." He was talking about the need for forgiveness and moving on.

IMPACT
RESOLUTION

This week, try to forgive someone who hurt you, and also try to forgive yourself for something you regret doing or saying. If you need to apologize to someone else who was affected by it, consider how you might do that. We are all human, which means we all make mistakes, but it also means we can forgive.

9

CLASS

Matt Majka was sitting in his office as the chief operating officer of the Minnesota Wild (NHL) on March 10, 2004. He had the TV on because the Minnesota boys' hockey tournament was underway. His office is connected to the Xcel Energy Center, where the Minnesota Wild play their home games. Whenever there was a close game or a game that went into overtime, Majka would get up and go watch the end of the game in person. He considered it one of the great perks of his job.

Now, before I go on with the story—if you are not from Minnesota, you might not understand what the state hockey tournament means to the people who live here. Our famous Land of Ten Thousand Lakes is the Land of Ten Thousand Frozen Lakes in the wintertime! Minnesota is also known as the State of Hockey, after all. The games are broadcast statewide, and I am thrilled to be a part of the broadcast team each year. They jam nineteen thousand fans into one of the best arenas in the country to watch two high schools battle it out on the rink. Here's all you really need to know: Neal Broten—who played in the NHL for seventeen seasons, won a Stanley Cup, won an NCAA championship, and was part of the 1980 Miracle on Ice team—says playing the state tourney for his high school in Roseau, Minnesota, is one of his top career highlights.

Matt Majka got over to the arena in time to see the underdog, Orono, go to overtime against Warroad, the defending class-A state champion and a city of just under two thousand people located only a few miles from the Canadian border. It is a town with a rich hockey tradition and is known as Hockeytown USA. The United States has only won two Olympic gold medals in men's hockey, and both times, there were players on those teams from the tiny town of Warroad, Minnesota.

T. J. Oshie gave Warroad the lead in the game in the first period when he scored a power-play goal. (Oshie himself went on to star for the American team in the Olympics in 2014 and was a key player for the Washington Capitals when they won the Stanley Cup in 2018.) As the spectators looked on, Orono tied the game at 1-1 in the second period. The game went to overtime. Majka had a front row seat to an instant classic at the Minnesota High School State Hockey Tournament.

Warroad was coached by Cary Eades, a man with quite a pedigree in hockey himself. He was a Canadian who helped lead his college hockey team at the University of North Dakota to two NCAA titles. He later was an assistant coach at UND and head coach for the Dubuque Fighting Saints in the United States Hockey League (USHL), whom he led to a National Junior Championship. Going into this state tournament as head coach at Warroad, he led the team to three state titles. Coach Eades was known as a tough, no-nonsense, competitive-to-the-core hockey coach. Believe me, no parents called him to complain about their kid not getting enough playing time!

Orono went on a power play early in the sudden-death overtime. (They had a one-man advantage for two minutes while the player who committed the penalty sat in the penalty box.) Ted Ylitalo scored the game-winning goal for Orono that day. The thrill of victory and agony of defeat were on full display in the arena and around the state on the live broadcast that day. Orono paid homage to Prince and partied like it was 1999! Warroad was simply crushed. Majka was watching it all unfold and marveled at the purity of high school hockey and the emotions it could muster in everyone involved. When things settled down, both teams lined up to shake hands, but he noticed something else extraordinary.

> *The thrill of victory and agony of defeat were on full display in the arena and around the state on the live broadcast that day.*

Warroad's Coach Eades walked over to the far net where the final goal was scored and picked up the puck. As he was going through the line to shake hands, he handed Ylitalo the puck and congratulated him. Majka happened to see it all unfold and could not believe the class and sportsmanship shown by this coach. Majka, who has been with the franchise for twenty years, said, "When people ask me about my top moments with the Wild, this is one of my top three!"

Cary Eades is now the head coach of the Fargo Force of the USHL. He described himself as the world's worst loser, especially after an overtime goal that meant their dream of a repeat was over. "It was a spur of the moment idea," Eades said. "I was devastated. On the way to console my goalie, I saw the puck in the net, and it flashed in my head to grab it because I thought the kid might want it."

"I still have the puck. It's in a frame," Ylitalo said. "For Coach Eades to think about it at a moment like that is incredible." He said as the years have gone by, it means even more to him today than it did back in 2004. Ylitalo said that his dad still talks about it. To bring these hockey stories full circle, he said he was watching the 2018 Stanley Cup finals with his young son. When they showed a close-up of T. J. Oshie, he told his son that he beat Oshie's team in a game in the state tournament. His son did not believe him.

Ylitalo also admitted that right before he scored the game-winning goal, he could have been called for a penalty himself for running into the opposing goalie. It was a close call. That would have changed everything and maybe even the result of the game. It also makes what Coach Eades did after the game even more remarkable.

IMPACT
RESOLUTION

When is the last time you witnessed a class act like that? Think about a time that you were self-less and made a first-class move when people least expected it. How did it make you feel? It doesn't have to play out on live TV for it to be impactful. Be inspired. Look for an opportunity this week.

10

CONNECTIONS

One of the main attributes of people who make an impact in their professional life is that they realize this fact: They are not in x, y, or z business. They are in the relationship business. The relationships you have with your customers, vendors, and coworkers will determine your success. It takes effort to seek new connections. You have to get to know people, find some commonality, and show them you genuinely care.

People want to buy from people they like. They like to eat at restaurants where they feel connected to the staff. They shop, bank, and bring their dry cleaning to people and places they feel connected to.

48

The best way to make those connections is by investing emotional capital. It can help you develop a bull market instead of just plain bull. Walt Disney used to say that there were three kinds of people in the world today: well poisoners, who discourage you and tell you what you can't do; lawn mowers, who are well-intentioned but self-absorbed; and enrichers, who are here to lift and inspire the lives of others. Enrichers are natural connectors.

Dan Stoltz, a client and good friend, is a person who breathes life into those around him. He is the CEO of Spire Credit Union, a nonprofit financial cooperative with almost one hundred thousand members. Dan might have set a record for being in the most parades in a two-year period. He was King Boreas Rex at the St. Paul Winter Carnival, and the very next year, he was the Minneapolis Aquatennial Commodore. Those are two major events, and with each one comes a commitment to promote the festivals for an entire year. Unconfirmed sources tell me that Dan got carpal tunnel syndrome from waving in hundreds of parades!

He is a world-class connector, and the main way he connects is through giving. It has an impact on his personal life, and it certainly doesn't hurt business either.

Dan's philosophy on life is to be a net giver, not a net taker. I guess it figures that someone in the financial business is going to worry about the net result, but the bottom line is this: Dan truly believes that to be rich, you have to give back. He says there are three T's that net givers have in their tool box: time, talent, and treasures. There are only twenty-four hours in a day, but when you give some of that time to a person or a cause, you make an impact. We all have different talents and use those talents to help others in various ways. Are you willing to give of your treasures to help others? Dan says your income doesn't matter. We all need to find a cause or a person to give to financially. Because Dan is very generous with his three Ts, he has been rewarded with great friends and amazing experiences. At Spire Credit Union, there has been an undeniable ripple effect. His team buys into the net-giver philosophy, which helps with company culture, and the company is developing a robust plan where employees can take paid time off to give back. People love to work for a company that truly cares about the community they serve.

> *People love to work for a company that truly cares about the community they serve.*

IMPACT
RESOLUTION

Dan also realizes the secret that net givers have figured out. It's good for the soul. How can you make connections by using your three T's? How can you become an enricher, a net giver, a connector? Identify one thing you can do this week to start building this into your personal and work life. Pretty soon, just like my friend, Dan Stoltz, it will be part of your DNA.

TRUST

The one piece of advice that I give to every young father is to always trust the instincts of the mother of their child. My wife, Laura, and I were at a picnic with our young son, Matthew, when he started vomiting. I thought we should take our sick kid home, but Laura turned to me and said, "We are going to the emergency room."

I started to drive to the hospital that was closest to our home, but Laura insisted that we go to Children's Hospital in Minneapolis. It turns out that Matthew was extremely dehydrated and needed emergency medical care in order to recover. I thought Laura was overreacting, but as usual, a mother's instincts are always right. I'm so glad I trusted her.

My friend and colleague David Horsager is the number-one expert on trust in the country, if not the world. He is the bestselling author of *The Trust Edge* and talks to Fortune 100 companies all over the globe. He says that a lack of trust is actually our biggest expense. The Trust Edge Leadership Institute has many teaching tools and coaching services that are geared toward helping companies and individuals, such as the Eight Pillars of Trust. Trust me, David knows his subject!

> *If you don't trust a friend, you cannot call them a friend.*

In his presentations and in *The Trust Edge*, David says, "Without trust, leaders lose teams. Without trust, people lose sales. Without trust, organizations lose productivity, relationships, reputation, talent, customer loyalty, creativity, morale, revenue, and results." That's a pretty loaded statement, but think of all the companies that have had security breaches where your personal information has been compromised. It cost those companies millions of dollars and customers they might never get back.

Think about your personal relationships. If you don't trust a friend, you cannot call them a friend. In many ways, trust is one of your greatest personal assets, partly because it is extremely difficult to get back. Don't take my word for it, take the teachings of His Holiness the Dalai Lama. "Friendship doesn't depend on fame, money, or physical strength. It's based on trust, and trust depends on love and affection."

Every year, Gallup polls for the most and least trusted occupations. Nurses have topped the list for sixteen years in a row! In 2017, military officers were next, followed by grade school teachers. As you might imagine, lobbyists, car salespeople, and members of Congress were the least trusted. If you were in a foxhole and could have one person next to you, would you want a nurse or a senator?

How important is trust? If you get a good baby-sitter who you can trust, are you willing to pay them a few more dollars an hour? Ask any parent and you will get an emphatic yes! Trusted people have a bigger impact because, just like that superstar babysitter, you are willing to trust them with your greatest assets. As you get older, you learn to judge people not by what they say but by their actions. That is how trust is earned.

IMPACT
RESOLUTION

This week, draw up a list of the five people you trust the most and examine why they are trusted. See what you might do to emulate them. Ponder how trustworthy you might be to others. What can you do more consistently that will raise your trust score with friends, family members, and colleagues?

12

INCLUSION

We live in a day and age where inclusion is needed more than ever. It's not just a buzzword in education. We've come a long way, but we still tend to make it too complicated.

When my daughter was eight years old, she had a big birthday party with a lot of friends to help celebrate, eat cake and ice cream, play games, eat cake and ice cream, and get silly. Did I mention they wanted to eat cake and ice cream?

A few months later, I was in a local grocery store when I was approached by a woman who asked me if I was Joe Schmit. I thought it must be one of the thousands (I mean, hundreds . . . or, more accurately, tens) of fans who watch me on KSTP-TV. It was none of the above. She asked me if I was Natalie's dad, to which I proudly said yes. She said that her daughter, Jillayne, could not stop talking about how much fun she had at the birthday party and how much she loved Natalie.

You see, Jillayne is confined to a wheelchair, and her mom said Natalie's party was the first one she had ever been invited to outside her own family. Natalie not only included Jillayne, but she also designed all the games and activities so Jillayne could participate. I wish I could blame my watery eyes on the dust in the grocery store.

Who owns the responsibility for inclusion? We all do. We need new ways to celebrate our differences, making the world our classroom. It teaches us to value diversity, which can build community. It's not just about disabilities, race, religion, equality, health, and education. It's about respect, tolerance, and values.

Inclusion can take many forms. Most people remember hockey coach Herb Brooks, who led a team of young Americans to a gold medal in the 1980 Olympics. It became known as the Miracle on Ice, which is also the name of a movie. But a lot of people don't remember that Herbie was also the head coach of Team

USA in the 2002 Olympics in Salt Lake City. The Americans won a silver medal, which was much better than most experts predicted the team would do in the Olympics.

Bill Robertson was the director of communications for USA Hockey and the liaison to the National Hockey League, since all the players in the Olympics were also pro athletes. He tells the story of how some representatives from Nike came in the team locker room and started handing out gift bags of merchandise to each of the players. It was like getting a swag bag at the Oscars. Coach Herb happened to walk in the room. He politely told them that unless they had merchandise for all of his staff, including the trainers, assistant coaches, PR staff, and equipment managers, none of the players would accept the gift bags. Nike scrambled to make sure that every member of the team, no matter what their role was, got a gift bag. Bill later saw Herbie give the security guards standing outside the locker room some things from his bag. As far as Herb Brooks was concerned, you were part of the team no matter if you could score a goal or not. It was an example of inclusion to make sure everyone was shown the same respect.

IMPACT
RESOLUTION

How can we be more inclusive? As leaders, are you including everyone in the discussion? This week, think of ways to honor and learn more about people who are not like you. Let your mind turn to people who play ambiguous roles. Their contributions can get overlooked. Who knows, you might learn something and make a new friend in the process.

13

GRATITUDE

Gratitude is a terrific sleep aid. Every night, in those moments before you fall asleep, try thinking of three things that happened that day for which you feel grateful. It works better than any over-the-counter medicine. Gratitude puts your mind in a good place—a place where those positive vibes can relax you. If you are ungrateful, you might sleep like a baby . . . and get up every three hours crying!

It's far too easy for people to concentrate on what they don't have instead of being content and grateful for what they do have. Brother David Steindl-Rast, an author and Catholic Benedictine monk, says it best: "In daily life we must see that it is not happiness that makes us grateful, but gratefulness that makes us happy."

If you have your health, start with that. We all have friends who have accomplished great things despite physical limitations or debilitating illness, and they still manage to be grateful. We had a producer who worked for us in the sports department for several years who was born without legs. He was victim to a drug prescribed in the 1960s to pregnant women who suffered from morning sickness, only to find out later that it caused birth defects.

Our producer, Dave Stevens, never let his disability slow him down or cause him to be bitter or ungrateful. He was a champion wrestler in high school. In college, he played NCAA Division III football and was listed in the program as three feet, two inches tall! Dave loved sports.

While at KSTP-TV, we never even thought about Dave's physical limitations because he would not have it. He was creative, talented, funny, and a little bit of a troublemaker. He was one of us. Dave eventually got a job on the assignment desk of ESPN, where he worked for twenty years. He is the father of three and is now a motivational speaker. In all the years I have known Dave, I have not ever heard him complain. He is grateful for all the opportunities that he worked for and that he received.

IMPACT RESOLUTION

Be thankful for the little things because someday you will find out that they are the big things. A gorgeous sunset, a good meal with friends, the joy of having a pet—those are the big things in life. This week, write down ten things that you are grateful for. If you have an accountability partner, share your list. Also this week, let a friend know that you are grateful for them and the little things they do. Grateful people innately understand the power of two very important words: thank you. People always say to look for the silver lining. When you are grateful, you will actually find it.

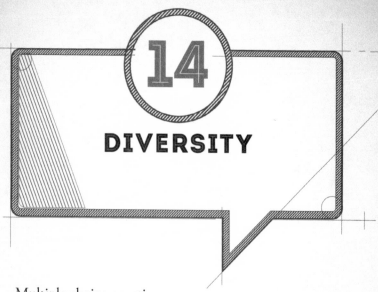

DIVERSITY

Multiple choice question:

Who said these words after years of traveling the world and meeting thousands of people? "I've learned that we are all pretty much alike. That no matter where you live, what you look like, what color you are, or what country you are from, we are pretty much the same."

A. Nelson Mandela

B. Maya Angelou

C. Oprah Winfrey

D. Willie Nelson

My guess is that all four of these people believed this, but it was spoken by Willie Nelson in an interview with Dan Rather on his cable TV show *The Big Interview*. We are all so much more alike than we are different, and that's why we need to celebrate diversity.

"It's okay to feel uncomfortable. It's the human condition," says my friend Morris Morrison, who was twice orphaned and left homeless and yet found a way to earn his master's degree. Morris is now one of the most in-demand speakers in the entire country. We have been friends for years, despite our differing backgrounds, and I am extremely proud of his achievements.

In one of our conversations, I admitted to Morris, who is African American, that I am a middle-aged white male who wants to celebrate diversity but sometimes finds it intimidating. I often find that I'm afraid of saying or doing the wrong thing. So I asked my friend for an example of who does diversity well. His response surprised me. He said, "Silicon Valley." He went on to explain that Silicon Valley cares about one thing: innovation. They don't care where the people or the ideas come from. They need talent, and the more diverse the talent, the better the chance they have to innovate. Different people with different backgrounds bring different and diverse ideas to the table. That is how they win the race in Silicon Valley.

That led me to ask Morris what we all can do, no matter what our race, religion, or geographic location, to honor others who are different from us. His first piece of advice was to engage. Talking to others will help break down your own walls.

Morris went on to give some simple tips that were very enlightening. He advises people to change the music they listen to on the radio. He says they should try rap, country, jazz, hip-hop, or some other genre they never listen to. Morris recalls a time when he was driving in the middle of nowhere. He desperately needed some music to keep him awake, but the only radio station he could get was country—which he hated. Morris eventually found himself liking country music. He says that we need to allow ourselves to be uncomfortable in order to break out of our culture of sameness. Even people who pride themselves on being open-minded need to switch the station once in a while!

> *Even people who pride themselves on being open-minded need to switch the station once in a while!*

DIVERSITY

Try a new restaurant where the customers don't look just like you and the food is unfamiliar. Follow a celebrity or politician on social media who is different from you and listen to what they have to say. Go to movies or watch shows on Netflix that are out of your normal genre. These are simple ideas that Morris says we can all do in order to expand our universe and learn to appreciate others who are different in one way or another.

This advice is coming from a man who recently got kicked out of a restaurant because of the color of his skin. Morris says it's okay if you aren't perfect at understanding how to navigate diversity in this world. Just continue to be genuine and have an open mind. Morris's best words of wisdom: "Never apologize for who you are, but never settle for where you are."

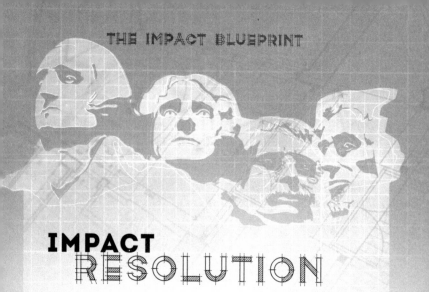

IMPACT
RESOLUTION

Make it a point to expand your horizons. Listen to new music, watch a movie or TV show that is out of your comfort range, make reservations for an ethnic restaurant that you have never been to, or talk to someone with a different background and listen. Celebrating diversity starts in your day-to-day choices.

15

GENEROSITY

Here's a question for you. Have you ever met a person who is generous and also miserable? When you do, be sure to let me know! People who make an impact in their corner of the world are generous. Sure, you can be generous with your money, but you can also be generous with your time, talent, knowledge, energy, or spirit. Each and every form of generosity is valuable.

In my first book, *Silent Impact*, I tell the story of Joe Mauer of the Minnesota Twins. When Joe was in high school, he invited a blind student to sit at his lunch table every day and would often walk this student to his next class. The impact of that simple, generous, and thoughtful act had a ripple effect that is still being felt to this day. When I asked Joe why he did it, his response was simple and powerful. He said, "I did it because it was the right thing to do."

Recently I was working with the leaders of Frandsen Financial Corporation, an interstate bank holding company that owns thirty-five community banks in Minnesota, Wisconsin, and North Dakota. Dennis Frandsen, owner and CEO, is a self-made man who never went to college, and he also happens to be an extremely generous person. Over the years, he made several donations to nearby Pine Technical and Community College.

> "I did it because it was the right thing to do."
> —Joe Mauer

While visiting the technical college, Dennis wanted to do more than just make another donation to the school. He decided that he would offer free tuition, plus a thousand dollars a year for books and supplies, to every graduating senior at Rush City High School. There are no strings attached. More than 40 percent of the graduates at Rush City will be attending college thanks to the generosity of this humble man.

The students will learn a trade and enjoy a career in a field such as nursing or computer science. There are many who could not have afforded postsecondary education without the help of Dennis Frandsen. Here's the kicker: when Dennis was asked in a local television interview why he did this, his answer was simple and powerful: "Because it was the right thing to do," he said. Where did we hear that comment before? The world would be a much better place if we all lived under the "because it was the right thing to do" mantra. Dennis is so tickled by the success of the scholarship program that he has expanded it to other high schools in communities served by his banks.

IMPACT
RESOLUTION

One of the great secrets about generosity is that the more you give, the more you get in return. A recent national study concluded that people who volunteer an average of six hours a week are happier, healthier, and more productive.

This week, plan to perform one generous act every single day.

16

DETERMINATION

Walt Disney was once fired by a newspaper because he wasn't creative enough. He later founded Disney World. Thomas Edison was considered not very bright by some of his teachers. After one thousand tries, he invented the light bulb. J. K. Rowling was on welfare as a failed writer until she wrote and published the *Harry Potter* series about characters from Hogwarts School of Witchcraft and Wizardry.

In each one of these examples, no one would have blamed them for giving up. They had relentless determination. We will all fail and make mistakes, but how we respond not only shows our character, but also builds character. It can be physically, emotionally, and psychologically challenging to ignore that inner voice that is begging you to quit.

You have probably heard or seen stories on Team Hoyt. Rick Hoyt was born in 1962 with cerebral palsy. His parents, Dick and Judy, were encouraged to institutionalize their son, but the Hoyts would not have it. They wanted their son to live as normal a life as possible.

When Rick was fifteen years old, he asked his dad if they could run a 5k race to help raise money for a lacrosse player who had been recently paralyzed. Dick was not a runner, but he agreed to the worthy cause. He pushed Rick in his wheelchair, and the pair finished second to last in the race. Rick told his dad of the amazing feeling he had during the race. He said he felt like he was running and completely forgot about his physical limitations. That was the start of a legendary racing career for Team Hoyt.

> *Determined people know there are no shortcuts to success.*

The father-son combination competed in over one thousand races including marathons and triathlons. The duo even biked from border to border in the United States in 1992, covering 3,735 miles in forty-five days.

They became celebrities at the Boston Marathon, where they ran thirty-two times!

Determined people know there are no shortcuts to success. What they might not realize is how many people they inspire with their example of determination and willpower. This is what I refer to as silent impact!

IMPACT
RESOLUTION

Think of a time in your life when you went the extra mile and how satisfying it was for you. As Chinese philosopher Confucius wrote about determination around 500 BC, "It does not matter how slowly you go as long as you do not stop." What single action could you take this week to raise your level of determination?

17

HOPE

Dr. Frank Pilney and his wife rented an RV and loaded up their thirteen children to make a big family road trip from Minnesota to ski the mountains of Montana. Little did they know, it was a trip that would change their lives and give hope to generations of children half a world away.

Before we head to the hills, let's talk about hope. Human rights activist and recipient of the Nobel Peace Prize Desmond Tutu said, "Hope is being able to see that there is light despite all of the darkness." Hope is such a powerful word because, without hope, you have hopelessness.

As the Pilney family was heading west for their mountain vacation, they stopped in Fargo, North Dakota, to go to Sunday mass at Nativity Church. The priest had just returned from Peru and asked the parish for help based on the needs he saw on his mission trip. He witnessed unfathomable poverty and many children being scorned simply because they were born with a cleft palate. Dr. Pilney happened to be a plastic surgeon. After mass, he gave the priest his card, and serendipity took over from there.

For the last thirty-eight years, Dr. Pilney has led pilgrimages to Peru to perform cleft palate corrective surgery on over six thousand children. The first year, only three people went on the trip. This past year, Dr. Pilney, who is eighty-three years old now, led a sixty-member team made up of volunteer nurses, an anesthesiologist, medical school students, and nine surgeons.

I asked Dr. Pilney why he continues to do it, and he said, "It's dramatic. In two hours, we can change their entire life." They give kids hope and a chance not to be outcasts in society. He said the biggest thrill is when the nurses take the babies after surgery and place them in their mother's arms. It's still emotional almost four decades later. One of his nurses called the journey "a vacation for the soul."

Dr. Pilney's charity is called Programa San Francisco de Asis (Program of St. Francis of Assisi) and it's completely run by volunteers. Everyone who goes on the mission pays their own way, plus they sacrifice personal vacation time. It's a trip of a lifetime, however; over half of the people who travel to Peru do it again and again. On the twenty-fifth anniversary of the program, a priest in Peru gathered the patients (then young adults) from the first year of the program to celebrate. It was an epic hug fest!

Dr. Pilney has taken all of his thirteen children and twenty-three grandchildren to Peru on this journey of love and hope. Think about the tremendous impact he has had on thousands of families who have gone from hopeless to hopeful.

IMPACT
RESOLUTION

This week, look for specific opportunities where you can offer hope and bring light to darkness. Think of times you were able to offer hope and how that made you feel. Offer words of hope to friends and colleagues when the opportunity comes your way.

18

EMPATHY

Empathy is not just feeling sorry for someone. It's feeling their pain and caring deeply about it. The difference between empathy and sympathy can often be measured by how much you listen. Empathetic friends will listen, and then they'll listen some more. They'll be so engaged in your pain, disappointment, or frustration that they feel some of it too.

My mother lived a wonderful eighty-four years on this earth. Her wake was in my hometown of Seymour, Wisconsin. The funeral director was my college roommate and one of my best friends in the world. I still often tease him that somebody with size 11 shoes must have just died, because he always seemed to have new shoes! A little mortuary science humor never hurt anyone.

At the wake, we formed a family greeting line. My two brothers and I were on one side of the casket, while my three sisters were on the other. Before I get to the point about empathy, I have to tell a funny story, and you have my permission to laugh. My brothers and I decided that since some of the people coming to the funeral home might be hard to recognize since we hadn't seen them in years, we'd help each other out by saying, "It's so good to see you, Mrs. Roberts." We thought it was a pretty smart way to avoid awkward moments.

As one elderly lady approached, my brother John followed the plan. "Oh, it's so good to see you, Mrs. Long. How are you?" To which she responded, "I'm vertical. It beats the alternative." She said that as my mother was lying horizontal no more than five feet away. My siblings and I started giggling and could not stop. It was like we were eight years old again. Humor can take the edge off awkward and emotional moments. It wasn't inappropriate; it was funny!

Here is what I observed about empathy and sympathy through the experience of losing my mom. I know it's always difficult to find the right words to say at a funeral, but I definitely learned what not to say. Please don't tell me how you felt when your mom died.

I know that it is all well inten-tioned, and we don't prepare people for how to act in times of grief. Have empathy for others and work to show it in a genuine way.

An empathetic person will make it about the person who is suffering.

An empathetic person will make it about the person who is suffering. Try some of these ques-tions or statements: What is the number one trait she gave to you? What are you going to miss the most? I wish I could have known her better.

You are showing your concern and making it about them, not about you. A good way to finish the conversation is to say, "I bet your mother was very proud of you and the person you have become."

IMPACT
RESOLUTION

Empathy is not a soft skill. It's something we can all learn to practice. Figure out ways to let people know you care. Show someone some empathy this week who has been needing a little extra TLC.

19

PATIENCE

Patience is not only possessed by those who come by it naturally. It's a skill that we can all work on. One of the first ways to grow in our capacity for patience is to recognize what triggers impatience. Once we recognize our weakness, we can develop some strategies that will make a genuine difference.

We are defined by how we respond to stress, anxiety, and adversity. We tend to either respond emotionally or intellectually. When we respond emotionally, we tend to react quickly, which is often accompanied by loads of impatience. When we respond intellectually, we usually exercise our patience muscle and the outcome is much better. To be blunt, responding emotionally is the lazy choice!

The next time you are upset and compose an email full of righteous anger, let the draft simmer overnight. Read the email the next morning, and nine out of ten times, you will be thrilled that you did not hit send the night before.

> To be blunt, responding emotionally is the lazy choice!

When my daughter Gaby and I traveled in Southeast Asia, we spent several days in Vietnam. It is where we witnessed the most incredible display of patience either of us had ever seen. In the large cities such as Hanoi or Ho Chi Minh City, the number-one mode of transportation is motor scooters. The combined populations of these two cities is twenty million people. My unofficial count of scooters was nineteen million! They were everywhere!

Here's what was unique. All the drivers blow their horns to let the people on scooters know that they are near. This is not done out of rudeness or impatience, as it is in the States. It's done as a courtesy to others on the road. We saw neither an accident nor even a hint of road rage. The locals collectively understood the rules of the road and the message of the horn. It is something that is hard to explain unless you see it in person.

As a side note, our tour guide in Vietnam had to give us a lesson on how to get across the street in a crosswalk. Basically, you should make no sudden changes in speed or direction and, no matter what, never stop moving. The motor scooter drivers will time your walk like a quarterback times a throw to a receiver. In other words, the phrase *stop dead in your tracks* could take on a literal meaning if you don't keep marching forward with a purpose!

When you feel yourself getting impatient, ask yourself if it will matter in a month. Will it matter in a week? How about in a day? Most of the time, the answer is no, so take a deep breath and try to develop habits that can turn patience from a weakness into a strength. We all need to get rid of clutter, and I am not talking about the clutter in our closet. I'm talking about the clutter in between our ears. Recognize your trigger points of impatience and figure out shortcuts to patience instead.

IMPACT
RESOLUTION

This week, keep a simple chart of wins and losses. Each time your patience is challenged, mark whether you responded emotionally or intellectually. Figure out if there are any commonalities in circumstances when you lose your patience. Maybe it's when you are tired or when your plate is too full. Once you identify the trigger, it becomes a lot easier to come up with ways to deal with the issue with a measure of patience and calm.

20

KINDNESS

"Don't mistake my kindness for weakness." It is a quote I have heard business people use, but I didn't realize until I did some research that it is attributed to Al Capone, the notorious gangster who was known as Scarface.

The famous mob boss was a despicable person, but he did have a point. Kindness is not a weakness. It is actually a strength. In today's confrontational society, I have news for you that is not fake news. It is easy to be mean. It's lazy and not very smart. Being kind sometimes takes effort.

Ellen DeGeneres is one of the most successful talk show hosts in television history. Sure, she is talented and funny, but one of the reasons for her major success is that she spreads kindness. She ends every show by saying, "Be kind to one another." She even has a shop of merchandise on the movement she started.

In an interview, she said, "Kindness is something we all have in us. It's not about making the world better for us. It's about making the world better for others."

You can tell that Ellen is genuinely kind and uses her immense platform to motivate and inspire people to show kindness in their everyday lives. Just imagine how much impact she has had on this world.

As we grow up, we all reach the stage when we figure out that giving a meaningful gift is much more rewarding than receiving one. It takes some of us a few more years than others to figure that out. It's very similar to the realization that it's a lot more rewarding to be kind than it is to be mean or degrading. This is why bullies are immature. They don't get it.

IMPACT
RESOLUTION

Kindness is considered a soft skill in the business world, but give me one trait that has more impact. Your goal this week is to do three random acts of kindness each day. Be creative and think small. Hold the door for someone. Carry an older lady's groceries to the car for her. Text a friend you aren't in the habit of talking to. Keep track of what you do and the response you get, if any. My guess is that you will have so much fun being kind that you will do it again next week.

21

HONESTY

Little white lies are still lies. We have so much to lose by lying that it's amazing how often we risk it. You can lose irreplaceable trust, respect, and friends. I guess that's why the old saying still works: "Honesty is the best policy." Believe it or not, that quote is attributed to a politician—Sir Edwin Sandys, an English politician and colonial entrepreneur, who said it in 1599.

Here's some breaking news about honesty. I no longer believe "Honest Abe" has the title of the most truthful person in US history. Kate Wynja of Sioux Falls, South Dakota, has that title now. Kate, an excellent golfer, had won state for the second straight year in the Class A Individual South Dakota Golf State Championship. As Kate was observing the posting of the scores, she realized that she had mistakenly written down a four for the eighteenth hole when she actually had a five. Had she originally recorded a five on the scorecard, she still would have won the title by a couple of strokes. Kate reported the mistake immediately, even though she knew the rules required her disqualification for turning in an incorrect scorecard. Kate gave up a state title because she was unwilling to be dishonest.

> We have so much to lose by lying that it's amazing how often we risk it.

To make the punishment even harsher, her disqualification cost her school the team state title. Kate told the newspaper in Sioux Falls, *Argus Leader*, "I knew I needed to tell them. It was really sad, mostly because I knew what the result would be. I knew that I would be disqualified and it broke my heart for the team. But I knew I couldn't leave without saying something."

By being honest, Kate Wynja lost a trophy but won so much more. Maybe it was summed up best by Don Swartos, the tournament director who had no choice but to disqualify Kate, when later that night he tweeted this:

"Wanted to cry for her, also wanted to cry because I was so proud of her integrity. I hope my own children grow up to have as much honesty and integrity as you, Kate. One of my new heroes and tough as nails."

Do you think Kate will ever have trouble with people trusting her? No way. We all know people who lie so often and so well that they don't even seem to realize they are lying. If someone like that has a prominent place in your life, weed them out. Limit your exposure to them whenever possible.

Today, our lives seem to play out on social media. One positive is that it keeps us honest because you never know when there will be a camera on you. It's tough to call in sick if someone posts your picture on Facebook at a concert that night.

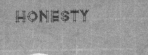

IMPACT RESOLUTION

This week, work on being honest with yourself. Be alert to white lies and exaggerations you might do out of habit. Watch for ways to practice your new commitment to honesty. Continue to be inspired by "Honest Kate."

22

CONFIDENCE

There is a fine line between being confident and being cocky. I covered Walter Bond when he was with the University of Minnesota basketball team. He played three years in the NBA, even though not one team thought enough of his talent to pick him in the draft after his senior season in college. Walter describes confidence in his motivational speeches as "arrogance under control."

Confidence is not walking into a room thinking you're better than everyone. Confidence is walking into the room and not having to compare yourself to anyone. I recently read an article featured in a blog by The Muse, an online career resource for job seekers and companies looking for talent. It gave tips on how to become the most confident person in the room. The ideas ranged from visualization to using more deodorant. It's hard to be confident with BO—Being Ordinary, that is . . . what were you thinking?!

Confidence comes through preparation. My daughter, Natalie, was a musical theatre major in college. When she was getting ready for a major audition, she would call me for a pep talk. To relieve the pressure Natalie was feeling, I would sing "I Have Confidence" from *The Sound of Music*. Just in case you think I'm a great singer, I assure you that I sounded like Mother Abbess on helium. Natalie would giggle every time. Actors, salesmen, and people in any profession—we all have to learn to accept and recover from rejection. It can play havoc with our confidence if we let it creep in.

Speaking of *The Sound of Music*, Oscar-winning actress Julie Andrews said in her memoir, *Home: A Memoir of My Early Years*, "The amateur works until he can get it right. The professional works until he cannot go wrong." The more you practice, the more confidence you will have. One of the most honest statements I ever heard from a professional athlete was from Gary Gaetti, a young third baseman for the Minnesota Twins in

1984. With only a few games left in the season, the Twins surprised a lot of experts by having a chance to make the playoffs. The Twins did not play well down the stretch, and in one particular game, Gaetti made a bad throw to first base that helped Kansas City win a crucial game. After the game, Gaetti said, "It's tough to throw the ball with your hands around your neck." He was implying that he choked from the pressure, a lack of confidence. By 1987, Gaetti was a confident all-star player who helped the Twins win their first World Series championship.

I know this makes me old school, but I am not a big fan of showboating in sports these days. I was a big fan of Walter Payton of the Chicago Bears. He scored 110 touchdowns in his Hall-of-Fame career, yet he never spiked the ball, did a dance, or taunted anyone. He simply handed the ball to the referee as if to say he was confident he would be getting back in the end zone again soon. Payton's impact made a ripple effect, and others, such as Larry Fitzgerald Jr. of the Arizona Cardinals, have his demeanor on the field too.

I used to think confidence was the eighty-year-old man who married the thirty-five-year-old woman and bought a house near the elementary school. That's a funny joke, but the reality is we could all benefit from a little more confidence. One of the best ways to grow in this, although somewhat counterintuitive, is to build others up. If you ever had a chance to coach youth sports, you know how rewarding it is to see the youngsters start to believe in themselves. When the kids lift each other up, their confidence soars to a whole new level. The same is true for adults. Affirmation is immensely effective, but

Affirmation is immensely effective, but the most magical part about it is that the one giving the compliment feels good and grows in confidence as well!

the most magical part about it is that the one giving the compliment feels good and grows in confidence as well!

When my daughters were six and eight, they started playing fast-pitch softball and were on the same eight-and-under team. Gaby was the youngest player on the team and was really struggling with making contact with the faster pitches. In her first at-bat, she actually lined up on the wrong side of the plate. At mid-season, Gaby did not have a hit to her name. Her coach Mike Rowecamp, the parents, and especially her teammates kept encouraging her. Suddenly, it all came together. Gaby lined a shot out to right field and had her first base hit! We were all so thrilled, as were her teammates, but I will never forget her coach. He was the happiest guy at the game. Mike built Gaby up over and over, and she eventually became an excellent hitter and had a lot of fun playing softball.

IMPACT
RESOLUTION

This week, let's all work on our confidence. Dick Bruso, an international speaker and executive coach, suggests to his audience: "Tune out the naysayers and tune in the cheerleaders." So be intentional about giving the cheerleaders in your life a more prominent voice. This will surely boost your confidence, but if you really get desperate, give me a buzz and I will belt out "I Have Confidence" for you!

23

FOCUS

Imagine this scene. Bill Gates and Warren Buffett are sitting together discussing life and business, and Gates's father gives the two billionaires a task. He asks them to both write down on a piece of paper the one thing that helped them the most in their careers. Without collaboration, they both write down one word: *focus*. If you are not focused, you are spinning your wheels. It's not just in business but in life too.

In the classic novel *Alice's Adventures in Wonderland*, Alice falls down a rabbit hole that transports her to a fantasy world. At one point when she is trying to get out, she has a handful of choices and does not know which one to take. Alice runs into the Cheshire Cat, who asks Alice where she wants to go. Alice says, "I don't much care where." The cat says that any road will take her there.

Thom Winninger, former president of the National Speakers Association, has given over three thousand presentations over the span of a forty-year speaking career. He uses that story from the classic novel when he speaks on the topic of focus. "Clarity in the moment comes from my ability to define where I am going," Thom says. If you have the end game in sight, you have a much better chance of success.

Thom says his speaking career took off as soon as he became laser focused on his area of expertise. He thinks people need to realize that there is a difference between variety and choice. Choices tend to be more thought out and variety tends to be more random. "Variety is different than choice. With choice you have clarity. The people with variety are typically confused," Thom says. It's something to consider in both life and business.

You know the people who say they can't move from their home because they have too much junk? According to Thom, if they use the choice-variety philosophy, they can easily solve the issue. He suggests you go around the house and label things with a numerical value of one, two, or three. Put a one on items you cannot live without, a two on items that you are willing to argue for, and a three on things you no longer need or want. Choice trumps variety in a tangible way and helps you gain focus.

> *Prioritize the one thing that will move you forward.*

There are more distractions than ever these days, so for people who have trouble with focus, Thom has some extremely practical advice. Prioritize the one thing that will move you forward. This will help you build momentum and not put too much on your plate. People who lose focus want to keep themselves from failure and mistakenly choose variety.

IMPACT
RESOLUTION

This week, think of a time when the entice-
ment of variety carried you away from your
focus. Then think of a time where you focused
on the choices that would help you reach your
goal. What is one thing you can do this week to
improve your ability to focus?

24

LISTENING

"Do You Hear What I Hear?" is a Christmas song that was written in 1962 and made popular by Bing Crosby. While it's a song heard over the holidays, I think that some people today would say *no* in response to the question posed in those lyrics. Listening is half of the communication process. Great listeners become great friends and great leaders.

Ever listen to the talking heads on TV or radio yapping about politics? It seems they are listening to no one but themselves. Do you finish other people's sentences? Are you the kind of person who cuts people off in a conversation? I love it when a husband or wife is telling a story at a gathering and the other one jumps in to either correct their spouse or to add flavor to the story. I mostly love it because that means it's not happening to me. Calling my wife out for not getting a detail just perfect is not kind and makes for a long ride home!

We should all try to be lifelong learners, and one of the best ways to do that is through listening. We have so many more options to listen and learn these days with podcasts and audiobooks. Even when we try to listen, sometimes we still hear it wrong. It is a skill worth working on. People use sayings or clichés wrong because they don't listen to what is correct. I just heard a radio interview where the person did not exactly say what he was trying to communicate. Instead of saying "for all intents and purposes," he said, "for all intensive purposes." It got a chuckle out of me.

Dr. Lyman Steil is the coauthor of a book called *Listening Leaders: The Ten Golden Rules to Listen, Lead & Succeed.* His research shows that listening is the most important skill for a leader to possess. He even says ineffective listening can have a negative impact on a company's bottom line.

Dr. Steil quotes the late, great Fred Rogers, who was not only an amazing communicator to children but was also known as a very focused leader. Mr. Rogers once wrote this about listening in his book, *The World According to Mister Rogers: Important Things to Remember.* "The purpose of life is to listen to yourself, to your neighbor, to your world, and to God and, when the time comes, to respond in as helpful a way as you can find." No wonder he received the Presidential Medal of Freedom, forty honorary degrees, and a Peabody Award!

We all have friends who are in love with the sound of their own voice. I have a friend who used to joke and say, "Now that I've talked about myself for the last half hour, why don't you talk about me for the next thirty minutes." If you have that friend, buy yourself a good pair of earbuds or otherwise avoid them!

IMPACT
RESOLUTION

Here is your goal for the week. Listen more than you talk. Focus intently on the conversation you are in and eliminate distractions. Work to be more aware of your need to be a good listener.

25

INSTINCT

If you told someone you hear voices, they would think you were nuts. The truth is, we all hear voices, which are known as our instincts. Those who learn to recognize and trust their instincts usually make better decisions than those who don't.

My friend Steve was in the hat business. He had contracts with all the professional sports leagues and the NCAA. It was a robust business with a lot of moving parts. He used companies he trusted to produce the quality he was looking for, including some manufacturers in China.

INSTINCT

Steve also ventured into negotiating exclusive rights to large events and Hollywood movies. He won the bid to produce hats in time for *Batman*, starring Michael Keaton, in 1989. He placed an order that was over one million dollars; it was the largest order in the history of his company. Normally, he would place the order over the phone and follow up with a fax or mailing with the artwork. Something inside told him that he should fly to China to meet with the company officials and oversee the production of his hat order. Those were his instincts, and thankfully, he did not ignore them.

> *Using your instincts and acting on those instincts are two completely different things.*

While Batman may be an iconic figure in America, the folks in China were not as familiar with the superhero. They were about to fulfill the large order of hats with the Batman logos upside down! Steve admitted that a million-dollar mistake would have been the end of his company. His ability to assess that a mistake would be a disaster saved his company and all the employees.

Using your instincts and acting on those instincts are two completely different things. At most Major League Baseball stadiums, local TV stations have several spots wired to the station where they can hook up a cable to a camera for live broadcasts. You may have seen the news trucks all park in one area where they can hook up to those cables for a live newscast.

In 1987, the Minnesota Twins made an unlikely run to the World Series. Every station in the Twin Cities was broadcasting live before and after the games. Our TV station's live remote position was the third-base dugout. Normally the engineer would have about forty feet of cable to set us up on the field for the live broadcast. But on the afternoon of game seven of the World Series, the engineer took the initiative to add an extra couple hundred feet of cable. He said we might need to move around more after the game.

That decision gave us a tremendous advantage when the game ended. We were out on the field with the players celebrating and getting live interviews. Meanwhile, the other stations were trying to talk people into coming over to their locked-down positions. Sometimes we ignore our instincts because we aren't sure they are spot-on. If something doesn't feel right to you, that is your instincts trying to give you wisdom.

IMPACT
RESOLUTION

If you have a friend who holds you accountable, have a discussion about a time you trusted your instincts and had a good result. Then turn the tables and see if either of you can think of a time when you did not listen to that inner voice and later wished you had. Your goal is to recognize that gut "feeling" and act on it when your instincts are trying to tell you something.

26

ACKNOWLEDGMENT

William James, an early psychologist and philosopher, famously said, "The deepest principle in human nature is the craving to be appreciated." We all have a need to feel valid and valuable. We all have a need to be acknowledged.

Here's a story that shows the power of acknowledgment. We'll call the subject Jordan to protect his privacy. Jordan felt unworthy, unwanted, and unloved. He spent twenty of the first thirty-five years of his life in juvenile detention centers and prisons. By the time he was five years old, Jordan was in the foster care system and was subsequently placed in seventeen different foster homes before aging out of the system. The assistant district attorney, Anne McKeig, who terminated his mother's parental rights three decades ago, never forgot him. It was not a job she relished, but Jordan's mother was battling serious drug, alcohol, and mental health issues, and his dad was not in the picture. Born with fetal alcohol syndrome, he was in an uphill battle.

Anne McKeig is now Minnesota Supreme Court Justice McKeig. One day, she was touring a particular prison in Minnesota when she recognized a picture on the wall; it was Jordan. Justice McKeig knew that he really never had a chance in life and was a victim of the system. She called his social worker and set up a meeting.

"Oh crap, what did I do now?" thought Jordan, as all previous appearances before judges were not good experiences. The meeting took place, went well, and lasted almost two hours. "I was shocked," he said, "Wow, this is just the opposite of what I was expecting."

Justice McKeig wanted Jordan to know that his mother loved him but was not capable of taking care of him. She needed all her energy just to survive. When Justice McKeig went on to tell Jordan that she cared about him too, he started to cry. He did not know anyone on earth cared about him. "I wanted to let him know that he has value, and he should feel worthy," Justice McKeig told me when recalling the meeting. She felt Jordan needed to be acknowledged to feel he had any value.

Jordan felt like he was just a number, not a person. As a matter of fact, he could rattle off his prison number as if it were his name. Justice McKeig wanted to make sure that he knew he wasn't just a nameless face. The system had failed him, and she would now be there to help support him. Justice McKeig refers to the story as "Wounded Knee" in honor of his heritage on the Pine Ridge Indian Reservation.

Jordan is now in a halfway house and feels like he has a new lease on life. He has a job and is learning to cope with life outside the prison walls. "This time it's different," he says. "I never felt like anybody cared, and now I have somebody in my corner. What more can I ask for?" He went on to tell me that Justice McKeig encourages him and that he is inspired and motivated to live a productive life.

Justice McKeig said, "It doesn't cost us anything to care." She said she was inspired by her mother, who always found time for kids who needed extra love and attention. Justice McKeig leaves every conversation or email with Jordan by telling him how proud she is of him and that she cares. Acknowledgement doesn't cost a thing, but in Jordan's case, it's priceless. The final chapter of his life is yet to be written, but the impact that one person made gave this man a fighting chance.

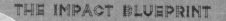

IMPACT
RESOLUTION

We all have a need to be appreciated and acknowledged. This week, look for opportunities to let people know you care about them, especially those who may feel invisible and unworthy. Helping someone feel worthy and acknowledged is an easy way to make an impact.

27

HUMILITY

The Mayo Clinic, located in Rochester, Minnesota, is one of the greatest medical institutions in the entire world. The clinic has treated kings, queens, and presidents because of its sterling reputation and cutting-edge research.

A friend of mine grew up in Rochester and told me a story about a friend's dad. He was a world-famous surgeon, but you would never know by the way he carried himself. One day, the surgeon was driving his son and his friend to a ballgame when they had to make a stop for gas. When they pulled up to fill the tank, an older man who was working under the hood of a car came to the doctor's vehicle to fill it with gas and wash the windows on the car. (For you youngsters out there, this is the way gas stations used to be. The gas station attendant would even check your oil levels. And by the way, this full service came with gas under a dollar a gallon.)

The mechanic had been working on an engine and had lots of oil and grease on his clothes and hands. He gave great service and made small talk while he did his job. After the doctor paid for the gas, and the mechanic went back to working under the hood of the automobile, the doctor turned to his boys and said, "Did you guys get a good look at that man? Well, we both have essentially the same job. We fix things that are broken, and he is probably as good or better at his job than I am at mine." That is humility, and the young boys in that car never forgot it.

I am aging myself here by recalling the song Mac Davis once turned into a hit that had the lyrics, "Oh Lord, it's hard to be humble when you're perfect in every way." We all know a few people who actually believe the song was written about them.

They think the world revolves around them, not the sun. As the saying goes, people with humility don't think less of themselves, they just think of themselves less. This makes me think of Dennis Ryan.

Dennis was hired in 1977 by the Minnesota Vikings to be the assistant equipment manager. He eventually was promoted to head equipment manager and is known as the hardest-working man in show business. When retired players come back to visit the Vikings, he's one of the first people they seek out because he was so good at taking care of the players.

In the summer of 2018, Dennis was named the Whitey Zimmerman Equipment Manager of the Year, an honor voted on by his peers across the NFL. Dennis did

Whether you are a surgeon, a mechanic, or a guy in charge of shoulder pads, jocks, and socks, humility is admirable.

not mention this award to anyone, and about a month after he received the honor, the Vikings PR department found out about it. They wanted to publicize it because it's really a tremendous accomplishment and honor. Dennis's first response was, "I guess I better tell my wife." When the story hit social media, Dennis gaveall of his assistants the credit. He was humble, hard-working, and heroic in the way he approached his job.

IMPACT
RESOLUTION

Whether you are a surgeon, a mechanic, or a guy in charge of shoulder pads, jocks, and socks, humility is admirable. This week, think of ways you can exude a spirit of humility to those around you. Try to notice when your ego gets in the way of being a person of impact. Not everyone needs to know what you accomplished or how much energy you spent doing it. Humility is an attractive trait.

28

ALTRUISM

My daughter, Gaby, has a passion for teaching children. She also loves to travel. Gaby was smart and motivated enough to develop a strategy to do both while she was earning her bachelor's of education at the University of Wisconsin. She was an exchange student in Australia, taught English to kids in Zanzibar, and did a mission trip working with children in Thailand. She was able to fund those trips by running several children's theatre camps in our basement and backyard when she wasn't at school or abroad.

I have always wanted to travel to Southeast Asia, so I made plans to join Gaby when she was done with her commitment in Thailand. We toured this wonderful country on a once-in-a-lifetime, father-daughter trip.

I am not going to give you a travelogue on our trip, but I will tell you what became very apparent during our visit there. Thailand must be one of the most altruistic countries on the planet. The people there are endlessly concerned about the well-being of everyone else, especially people visiting their country. It so happens that 94 percent of the country's population is Buddhist. I am not an expert on Buddhism nor the topic of reincarnation, but our experience in the country was overwhelming.

Most Buddhists believe in samsara, the never-ending cycle of birth and death. They believe samsara is governed by the law of one's own karma. Good conduct produces good karma, and bad conduct produces evil karma. Gaby and I experienced example after example of the Thai people practicing good karma.

The Thai people were 100 percent concerned about our experience in their country. They exuded niceness and graciousness at every turn. Whether it's a waiter, bellhop, cab driver, or tour guide, tips are not expected in Thailand. When we did give someone a tip, no matter how much, they accepted the money with both hands and bowed in gratitude and respect. The size of the tip had very little to do with their reaction. They only cared about seeing a happy customer.

We became very aware that the people who worked in customer service were not working us over for a tip. Believe me, we have all been in situations where someone pours out the fake enthusiasm to make sure they get a big tip. This was never the case in Thailand, whether we were in a huge metropolitan city like Bangkok or in a small village like Phuket. I found myself giving larger tips in Thailand than I do in the United States. It was a natural outpouring of our gratitude.

Gaby and I took a journey halfway around the world and learned a very important and unexpected life lesson. The well-being of others is equally or maybe even more important than our well-being. Valuing others above yourself involves acts of selflessness. Even better is when it is done without any fanfare or expectation.

I used to work with a highly successful businessperson who would say, "Cash follows creativity." That might be true, but I think some of the most successful businesses are truly altruistic. Take care of the customer, listen to them, give them what they want, and profit will never be in short supply.

IMPACT RESOLUTION

How can you practice altruism this week? Reach out to a friend just to let them know you care. Volunteer your time, talent, or resources to someone or an organization. As a leader, schedule yourself fifteen minutes a day to go around to compliment people and reward progress. Kick yourself whenever you think about yourself before you think of others.

29

LEGACY

July 12, 1996, in a steamy, jam-packed room in the bowels of the Hubert H. Humphrey Metrodome, the legendary Minnesota Twins superstar, Kirby Puckett, announced his forced retirement due to glaucoma taking the vision in his right eye. Puckett was still in his prime and arguably the most popular athlete in Minnesota history. His teammates from the Minnesota Twins, the front office, and even members of the media were all emotional. It was a moment none of us will ever forget.

Puck, as he was known, handled the news conference like it was a hanging curveball. He knocked it out of the park. "Tomorrow is not promised to any of us," Puck said. I had probably heard something similar to that quote no less than one hundred times, but never had it meant so much. Today that quote is prominently displayed in the Twins clubhouse so every player can see it every day. It's a reminder that life is fragile and nobody is immune to challenges, obstacles, or heartbreak.

Most of us look toward leaving a legacy after our death, but what about leaving a legacy while we are still alive? Legacies have nothing to do with how much money or personal property we leave for our heirs; they have to do with what emotional equity we have imparted on our loved ones and all who knew us. The old, popular Jewish proverb says, "The only true dead are those who have been forgotten." In other words, you die twice. Once when you physically leave this world and once again when people quit talking about you.

I hate to get morbid here, but if we all spent a little time thinking that tomorrow is not promised to any of us, we might all live with more love, respect, and patience. Maya Angelou said, "Your legacy is every life you touch." If they have to use your resume as eulogy material, you did not lead a life of significance.

There has been a lot written and plenty of research on the regrets of dying people. Bronnie Ware is widely respected because of her work in palliative care with people who are near the end of their lives. She said the most common regrets people have are that they worked too hard, didn't spend enough time with their friends, and didn't have the courage to be true to themselves about what they needed to be happy. She's written a book on the subject called *The Top Five Regrets of the Dying* if you are interested in learning more. We all have regrets in life, but we can start rewriting our obituary today by striving to live a life of impact. Jackie Robinson, the baseball player who broke the color barrier, has a famous quote that speaks to the core of this book: "A life isn't significant except for its impact on other lives."

IMPACT
RESOLUTION

What would your legacy be if your life were suddenly cut short? What is your living legacy today? What can you do today to help avoid future regrets? These are excellent questions that everyone should discuss with their spouse, good friend, or accountability partner. This week, think of just one thing that you can do that will help you improve your legacy.

30

RESPECT

The late, great Aretha Franklin was right when she belted, "R-E-S-P-E-C-T. Find out what it means to me." To most people, that seven-letter word means the world. People will have different opinions, and it's not realistic that we would agree on everything. Life is certainly easier when we respect other ideas and thoughts. I know it's tough, but if you *really* want to have an impact, show respect to people who don't deserve it. It's not a reflection on their character; it's a reflection on your character.

I do not like to get political because the discourse is so tainted these days, but we have a shining example in the late senator and American hero John McCain and former senator and vice president Joe Biden. They were from different parties and were far apart from each other on almost every issue. However, they respected each other. Even though their approaches and ideals were different, they had the dignity to maintain respect for each other. They were true friends who happened to be on opposing teams. One time, members of both political parties got upset at the senators because they would sit next to each other instead of with their own party-line colleagues. They realized that compromise did not mean defeat. Other politicians could learn from these two men, couldn't they?

Here's an easy way to show respect. Do you know the names of the security guards at your company, the custodians at your church, the parking lot attendants, the baggers at your grocery store, or the service workers at your favorite gas station?

I have the utmost respect for Bart Starr, Hall of Fame quarterback and former head coach of the Green Bay Packers. I was a kid who grew up thirteen miles from Green Bay when Bart led the Pack to victories in the first two Super Bowls. Bart was the MVP of those two games and cemented his hero status in the state of Wisconsin.

While I was a fan of Bart as a player all along, I became a fan of Bart as a man when I covered him in the early '80s when he was coaching the Green Bay Packers. To be honest, he was not a very successful coach, but he was a man of strong character. I had total respect for him because he showed respect for everyone, even a pup reporter like me who was trying to figure out his place in the TV business. I wrote a couple of stories about Bart in my first book, *Silent Impact*. He was a man who talked the talk and walked the walk.

A few years back, I gave a speech at Lambeau Field. Unfortunately, it was in one of their meeting rooms, not to a full house on the frozen tundra. After the presentation, I went to visit some old friends in the Packers' front office and was able to get Bart's address. I hadn't talked to him in years and wanted to send him a copy of my book. I mailed the book no more than five hours before I heard that Bart had a stroke and was facing some very serious health concerns. I wanted so badly to retrieve the book out of the mail and send a get-well card instead!

About three weeks later, I got the most beautiful letter from Cherry Starr, Bart's wife. She thanked me for the book and wanted to make sure I knew that Bart was fighting hard and staying positive through his health struggles. Then she wrote, "I read the stories to him that you had in the book and you should have seen him light up." I was stunned and happy that without trying, I had a positive impact on a man who had a big impact on me so many years ago.

IMPACT
RESOLUTION

Who do you respect? Think about why you respect him or her. Try making a short list so you can mark the things you'd like to work to acquire. You'll be amazed at what some intentionality will do in developing this trait!

31

RESILIENCY

Michael Jordan, one of the greatest if not *the* greatest basketball player ever, got cut from his high school team. He missed nine thousand baskets, lost over three hundred games, and missed twenty-nine shots that would have won games at the buzzer had he made them. Jordan went on to become a six-time NBA Champion, five-time MVP, and fourteen-time NBA All-Star! Every kid who laces up a pair of Air Jordans wants to be like Mike. Sure, he had amazing skills, but besides world-class athletic skill, Jordan was famous for his resiliency. "Obstacles don't have to stop you. If you run into a wall, don't turn around and give up. Figure out how to climb it, go through it, or work around it," Michael Jordan once said when talking about the importance of mental toughness.

We've all heard that it's not whether you get knocked down but how you get back up that counts. That's what being resilient is all about. As parents, we love to teach our kids how important this skill is and then sometimes forget to practice it ourselves. People who are resilient are both optimistic and smart enough to know what they can control"and

> *They look at adversity as a chance to learn and grow or even change.*

what they cannot control. They look at adversity as a chance to learn and grow or even change. This is easier said than done!

Dick Enrico is a serial entrepreneur from Minnesota who likes to call himself an "occupational opportunist." In 1992, he started selling used exercise equipment and struck gold. He called his company 2nd Wind Equipment, and at its peak, he had just over one hundred stores spread out over eleven states. He was famous for his off-the-wall TV spots and his on-the-wall advertisements in public bathrooms. He could write a book on guerrilla marketing. Here's a guy who never stepped on a treadmill in his life, yet he was the owner and spokesperson for a company that sold thousands of them. He eventually sold the company after twenty years of unconventional marketing and business tactics.

Everybody thought Dick Enrico was an overnight success, but nothing could be further from the truth. He was not only a serial entrepreneur, but he was also totally resilient. Before he hit it big with 2nd Wind Equipment, he sold pots and pans door to door. As a matter of fact, he started at least twenty companies, such as storage sheds with thatched roofs, waterbeds, and car phones, and none of them ever made it to the New York Stock Exchange. Some of those ventures were downright disasters. Dick told me, "They were not failures, they just lacked success." When he turned 2nd Wind Equipment into a big success, the *Wall Street Journal* did a profile on him with the headline, "Try, Try Again."

What people did not understand about Dick is that in every business that did not make it, he learned valuable lessons in the art of the sale. He made a good living selling pots and pans as a door-to-door salesman. He describes himself as very street smart and an exquisite closer. It was Dick's resiliency that helped him sell over one billion dollars of exercise equipment!

Now in his seventies, Dick is on to a new technique he calls SCAM (sales, creativity, and marketing). He has opened 2nd Shade Patio Furniture, which is replicating the successful model he used at 2nd Wind. One of the keys to Dick's success and resilience is his ability to take risks and change if things aren't working. "I can spin on a dime," Dick says. And it runs in the family. Dick's brother, the late Roger Enrico, was former CEO of PepsiCo.

When the going gets tough, do you get going or do you get lost? Do you bend but not break? Think of Michael Jordan and Dick Enrico. If you don't fail once in a while, you are playing it too safe.

IMPACT
RESOLUTION

With a good friend or accountability partner this week, discuss a time where you had to dig deep and because of it you not only survived but thrived. Make a mental note every time resilience helps you accomplish something. Maybe you need to develop thicker skin when it comes to criticism or failure. Maybe you need to be more willing to take and use constructive feedback. Maybe you are getting no feedback and need to solicit some. Whatever it is for you, growth in this area will surely impact your future success. You know what else is true? The harder you work, the luckier you get. Don't give up!

32

LET IT GO

Elsa in the Disney classic *Frozen* is so right. If you have young kids or grandchildren, you know the lyrics by heart, so go ahead and sing them with me. "Let it go, let it go. Turn away and slam the door." What are your barriers to letting go? Do you have a hardship in your life that makes letting go especially difficult?

Just because our past is not perfect, doesn't mean our future can't be something to be very proud of. Sometimes there are imaginary hurdles that we need to leap over.

Norman Lear is one of the most influential producers in television history. He was the mastermind of groundbreaking shows like *All in the Family*, *The Jeffersons*, and *Sanford and Son*. Just a few years ago, when he was ninety-three years old, a documentary of his life and career was coproduced by American Masters series and Loki Films in 2016. *Norman Lear: Just Another Version of You* is an intimate look at his life, the risks he took in his career, and the regrets that he still carries with him.

Norman did not have a good relationship with his father, who went to prison when Norman was nine years old, and it still bothered him over eight decades later. In the documentary, he says something undeniable and enlightening. He says that you and you alone are responsible for your own happiness. It's as if the interview itself was another step in Norman's journey of coming to terms with this lifelong, imaginary hurdle.

Joe Calloway, a legendary leadership development speaker, thought leader, and author of many books, spoke from the main stage at the National Speakers Association convention. Two thousand successful speakers were his audience. What in the world would he have to say to them? Joe told them about one big business mistake they were likely making: spending too much time on their to-do lists and not enough time on their let-go lists.

LET IT GO

What are you holding onto in your business or your personal life that is keeping you from progress or success? Whether you are holding on out of habit or out of fear, you need to be brave and let it go!

We are all human beings. Sometimes letting go is not an easy job. We make mistakes, but we also choose whether to blame someone else and hold on or whether to forgive ourselves and move on. As Will Rogers once said, "Good judgment comes from experience, and a lot of that comes from bad judgment."

IMPACT
RESOLUTION

This week, think of something you've been holding on to and work toward letting go of it. It will feel *so* good. Forgive someone, forgive yourself, or admit that negative energy is damaging you and others around you. If you are having trouble, listen to Elsa sing the famous Disney song. You'll be inspired.

33

PASSION

When perseverance combines with compassion and you add a scoop of tenacity, you get an unbeatable force of passion. Steve Jobs had unparalleled passion, and with that, he changed the world. So did lesser-known Jason McElwain and his passionate coach, Jim Johnson.

Coach Johnson was the head basketball coach at Greece Athena High School near Rochester, New York. Three years in a row, Jason McElwain (J-Mac) tried out for the team, and three years in a row he was cut. Even though J-Mac did not make the final roster, he stayed on as the team manager for all three seasons. Among other amazing qualities, J-Mac has autism. He was an attentive and energetic manager who inspired the team in many situations. Coach even let him say a few words to the team after each practice!

This was Coach Johnson's twenty-fifth year of coaching, and he was still looking for his first section title in New York. He had led his team to the section semifinals six times but could not get over the hump. When J-Mac talked to the team, his personal mantra was to help the team win their first section title. He said it in his frequent pep talks to the team. The coach made his dedicated manager a promise. If he continued to do a good job, J-Mac could suit up for senior night and maybe even get in the game.

When perseverance combines with compassion and you add a scoop of tenacity, you get an unbeatable force of passion.

The crowd was buzzing on senior night before the game because word got out that J-Mac might get a chance to play. With 4:19 on the game clock, Coach Johnson looked down the bench and told J-Mac that he was going in. What happened next changed the lives of Coach Johnson, the players, and many other people.

J-Mac took his first shot. He missed the hoop, the net, and the backboard. Air Ball. Then he missed his second shot. Coach Johnson was hoping his decision would not backfire or be embarrassing for J-Mac. What happened next can only be described as a miracle. J-Mac hit a three-pointer. Then he made another. Then he made another. He scored twenty points in the final three minutes! That is something NBA star LeBron James could accomplish, but a kid who could not even make the team? It was positively magical. As the game ended, the student body rushed onto the court and J-Mac was carried off as a hero. It brought tears to the eyes of the parents of both teams. Watch the story on YouTube, and I dare you not to get emotional.

The night Jason McElwain became the big man on campus happened twelve years ago. Now that some time has passed, I asked Coach Johnson for his perspective on the most rewarding night of his coaching career. He said that the local newspaper wrote an article about the game, but the focus was on the team winning the game and not J-Mac's contribution. (I might have fired that reporter, just saying!) When someone informed the local TV stations that there was video of the game, they all came out and did a feature story. The news spread from Rochester to Richmond to Rome in record time.

Coach was surprised by all the attention, but when he looks back, he is happy and proud that the team kept passing J-Mac the ball. He did not tell the kids to do that; they were following their own instincts. Three weeks after this momentous night, Coach Johnson finally won his first section championship. "I don't know if we would have won that title without the J-Mac night," Jim said. "It united our team for the playoffs."

Whenever I see a story on how a student with physical challenges or special needs gets in a game to score a touchdown or score a goal, I think that movement started with this special night in 2006. It also helped raise awareness for autism. Jason McElwain's passion for basketball and Jim Johnson's compassion for mentoring young athletes changed many lives that night.

IMPACT
RESOLUTION

Is there someone in your circle of influence who faces particular challenges? Do one specific thing this week to encourage him or her in an area where they've demonstrated passion. It could be the spark they need.

34

SINCERITY

One of my closest friends happens to be one of the highest performing salespeople in the country. Phil has had a long, successful career in sales, so naturally I turned to him when I was preparing a presentation for a sales group. I asked him about his secret to success.

Phil said, "Joe, the key to success in sales is sincerity . . . and once I learned how to fake that, making sales was easy." We both laughed, and I realized that Phil's sense of humor and his relationship-building skills were the real keys to his success.

I got busted one time with fake sincerity. Let's be honest, we all do this sometimes so we don't disappoint people. I ran into someone who started talking to me like we were long-lost friends. I played along with it, hoping that something he said would trigger a memory so I could figure it out in time to save face.

Nothing did. At one point, he stopped talking and said, "FE." I asked what he was talking about. He replied, "Fake enthusiasm, that's what you have." He could tell that I had no idea who I was talking to, and he busted my chops good. We eventually laughed about it when he told me he was a former college football player that I had covered fifteen to twenty years earlier. I sincerely blew it. Nobody wants to be called or perceived as a phony, and I never want anyone to ever say FE to me again. When you are sincere, people can tell.

Bob Schlichte, marketing guru for Grand Casinos in Minnesota, has come up with creative promotions, programs, and strategies to take special care of their best customers while they continue to grow and develop new clientele. Bob says he started realizing that the key to good business is sincerity. He says it's like building a ship: partnerships, relationships, sponsorships, mentorships, and friendships are all a part of building good business. Bob is about as genuine as they come, and one thing is for sure: nobody ever accused him of fake enthusiasm.

IMPACT RESOLUTION

This week, try to figure out a way to make sincerity a priority. If you aren't used to it, you might feel uncomfortable. How can you best show concern and understanding and hold genuine intentions? Sometimes it's just a matter of spending some quality time with someone.

35

PURPOSE

Mark Twain is often quoted as saying, "The two most important days in your life are the day you are born, and the day you find out why." The great American writer, humorist, and lecturer certainly knew that discovering your purpose is not easy and an important journey.

Ann Tillotson was a high-power investment banker for Piper Jaffray, an international full-service investment bank and asset management firm based in Minneapolis. Ann decided to leave the financial industry to be a stay-at-home mom when she and her husband had the first of their two children. She also knew that she did not want to be the kind of stay-at-home mom who was only concerned about her children. She wanted more. Ann was a go-getter and determined to find a way to make a difference.

> "The two most important days in your life are the day you are born, and the day you find out why."
> —Mark Twain

One of the many volunteer opportunities that Ann was involved with was serving lunch at her son's elementary school once a week. In 1996, she noticed that when some kids arrived at the checkout register in the school cafeteria, the register would give the lunch lady a message. The lunch lady would take the hot lunch tray and substitute it with a peanut butter and jelly sandwich. Ann inquired and found out that the student didn't have enough lunch money.

Instead of being upset at the school or sad about the situation, Ann was determined to do something about it. No one could stand in Ann's way when she had a purpose. She found out that 40 percent of the students at their elementary school qualified for free and reduced lunch. She also learned there was another category of students whose parents did not quite qualify for government funding but still could not afford to pay for hot lunch. Some had illness in the family or a car repair bill that was causing financial stress.

Ann went to the principal, Tom Lee, a solid leader and a good man. His mantra was, "If it's good for the kids, then let's do it." On her own, she quickly raised $1,200 and the problem was solved for the rest of the school year. "All you had to do was see the look on their faces when they were denied hot lunch. No one would have the heart for that." She realized that on top of being hungry, the kids were also embarrassed.

Soon Principal Lee talked to other elementary school principals in the district and found out it was a universal problem. Ann worked with the principals, the superintendent, and other concerned parents. They started raising the necessary money to cover the accounts that were below zero. Today, the program is called Children's Food for Thought. It's not only in every elementary school in Bloomington but in every middle school and the two high schools as well. So far, the organization has covered the cost of fifty thousand lunches with over $110,000.

Ann's sensitivity and perseverance have made a lasting impact. Hunger is a real problem in America today. As Ann demonstrated, when you find a purpose and use your talents to serve that purpose, you can move mountains. Ann described her leadership on this issue like this: "The real gift was to do it for those who could not do it for themselves." Not surprisingly, Ann now serves as the president of the Education Foundation of Bloomington, Minnesota.

IMPACT RESOLUTION

Do you have a sense of purpose? If you struggle with this, be inspired by Ann's example. Look for problems to solve, use your talents, listen to your heart, engage with others who can help, and above all, take action. This week, have a conversation with a friend and share your sense of purpose.

36

VISION

Anytime Fitness is the McDonald's of twenty-four-hour fitness centers. With over four thousand franchise locations in thirty countries, Anytime Fitness was ranked first by *Entrepreneur* on its 2015 global franchise list. Many others have tried to copy the business model, but none have had equal success because they did not have the right vision.

The three original owners of Anytime Fitness had all been in the health and fitness industry. They saw a need and had the vision and the guts to take a risk to fix it. Within seven years, they had a thousand franchises all over the United States. They also had private equity firms offering the founders enough money for the company that they could all retire and never work again.

One of the three original owners wanted out, so Chuck Runyon and Dave Mortensen took the risk of buying him out while still saying no to the millions being offered by the investors. Most people would not have the cojones to know that the deal they just signed carried an interest payment of $13,000 a day. But Chuck and Dave had not only a vision for what the company could be but also a plan they were willing to execute. They are now working on opening a center in Antarctica, so they will become the first franchised business to operate on seven continents.

I was preparing to speak to this dynamic Minnesota-based company. Before anyone works with Anytime Fitness, Chuck and Dave have them read their book, *Love Work*. It outlines the game plan they used to create their health club success. Their core values are based on what they call the four Ps: people, purpose, profits, and play. They also make a promise to every employee that they will never have to miss life's important moments.

That commitment builds loyalty with employees and causes other companies to be jealous. At last count, there were around four thousand employees and members who have a tattoo of the company logo somewhere on their bodies. When you combine a strong vision with a crystal-clear plan and build a team by caring for them, you build a tattoo-worthy brand.

"The only thing worse than being blind is having sight but no vision." This famous quote from Helen Keller reminds us that a vision without a plan is just a fairy tale.

Speaker Doug Stevenson says the best thing you can do is "pick a date." If you want to take dancing lessons, learn how to play guitar, or program robots, you have to pick a date. Sign up for a class or buy a book and do some self-study. Too many of us talk about our goals, but if you have a vision for what you want to become, pick a date and make it happen!

IMPACT RESOLUTION

What is your vision? Are you willing to take a risk to accomplish your vision? Maybe it's a new job, a new hobby, or some area of self-improvement. Your task this week is to pick a date, make a plan, and make it happen. You don't have to get a tattoo, but it's always a possibility.

> *Are you willing to take a risk to accomplish your vision?*

37

SCRAPPY

"Hey yo, I'm just like my country / I'm young, scrappy, and hungry / And I'm not throwing away my shot." That's from the amazing Broadway musical *Hamilton*. Lin-Manuel Miranda wrote both the music and lyrics to "My Shot," where his character, Alexander Hamilton, is expressing his dreams and passion for the revolution. Anyone leading a revolution is bound to be scrappy.

Being scrappy is the ability to dig deeper than you normally do. It's a mental toughness and grit that allows you to take risks yet stay on your feet. In today's competitive global economy, there are some people in business who think that being scrappy is even more important than your education or your experience.

In hockey, when the puck goes into the corner and two players on opposite teams go after it, the player who comes out of the scrum with the puck is the winner. This is a battle of will, and 90 percent of the time, the scrappiest player wins. I remember covering former Minnesota Vikings linebacker Jack Del Rio before he became a successful NFL coach. Jack was describing one of his teammates and gave him the ultimate compliment. "If I'm in a foxhole, I want him next to me because he's scrappy." I never forgot that quote.

Steve Levitan is the cocreator and executive producer of the highly successful ABC television series *Modern Family*. I happened to be one of the forty-two thousand people in attendance at Camp Randall Stadium in Madison, Wisconsin, in May of 2017 when Levitan was the commencement speaker for the 6,300 graduates. His message was that nobody will remember your failures, and that the only way he was able to turn from TV reporter to successful producer of television comedies was being scrappy.

Levitan told the young graduates to take risks while they were young and that their passion would get them through their failures. He said before he was part of one of the most successful sitcoms in television history, he had written nine sitcoms that failed, and some failed miserably. "Now, gratefully, I'm introduced as the cocreator of Emmy-winning *Modern Family*," Levitan said, "and no one remembers I'm the idiot who failed nine times in a row."

There's an old adage that says the harder you work, the luckier you get. As mentioned in *Esquire's The Meaning of Life: Wisdom, Humor, and Damn Good Advice from 64 Extraordinary Lives* by Ryan D'Agostino, Oscar-award winning actor George Clooney said, "The best lesson my mom ever taught me was how to be scrappy."

IMPACT
RESOLUTION

How can you become scrappier when it comes
to chasing your dreams? This week, think about
a time you dug deep and came out with a win.
How did it feel? What is one area of passion
where you could take a little risk and put
your resilience to the test? Be scrappy, rinse,
and repeat.

JOY

You might be wondering why joy would be an Impact Resolution when we already had a section on happiness. I have to admit, I always lumped them in the same category too. However, psychologists and human behavior specialists say they are different, and I can see why. Happiness tends to be external, based on people, places, things, and events. Joy is an internal feeling that comes when you make peace with who you are and how you are. It comes from a deeper place and is longer lasting. Experts say that joy is stronger and not as common as happiness.

From 1987 to 1991, I had the great pleasure of working with a news reporter at KSTP-TV by the name of Steve Hartman. In my over thirty years of TV news, I have never worked with a better writer. Steve could tell a story about grass growing and it would captivate people to the end.

If you recognize the name, it's because Steve took over the "On the Road" segment from Charles Kuralt on *CBS News* in New York. Steve comes to mind often. As a matter of fact, he has done stories on two of the people I wrote about in this book: Coach Jim Johnson and Judge Chris Wilton.

If you are not familiar with Steve's stories, google him. They are all amazing and are very positive. Steve told me that his goal on every story is to bring joy to people. "News does a good job at anger but does a terrible job at bringing overwhelming joy," Steve said. He knows he has hit the joy button when he brings "happy tears" to the viewers. I'm telling you, nobody is better at it. Nobody!

So how does Steve pick his stories to tell? First of all, if it's a pitch from a public relations firm, he doesn't even listen. He wants the motive to be pure. Secondly, he says he wants to do a story on someone who is better than he is. That's Steve's humble way of saying he knows that if he is inspired by the story, he will be able to tell it in a way that it will inspire others.

Besides bringing joy, Steve said that most of his stories have two traits in common: kindness and optimism. He also said that those traits do not have an age limit. He has done stories on everyone from four-year-olds to centenarians.

In a recent conversation with Steve, I reminded him of my favorite story he did when he was at KSTP-TV. It was about a blind man who wanted to learn how to swing. Not only did Steve teach the young man how to swing, but it was one of the most popular stories ever at the station and had a profound impact on his career.

A veteran investigative reporter, who was a pretty hard-core journalist at the station, came up to Steve after that story and said something like this: "It's too bad, kid." Steve thought for a second that the news-hound hated the story, but then he said, "It's too bad that you just did the best story of your career at such a young age!" It helped Steve discover that his gift was as a feature reporter. We call that Silent Impact. And by the way, that old journalist was wrong; Steve would go on to tell hundreds of stories just as good if not better than that one.

IMPACT
RESOLUTION

The late Zig Ziglar, one of the world's most-quoted motivational speakers, once said, "True joy comes when you inspire, encourage, and guide someone else on a path that benefits him or her." People who make an impact look for ways to cultivate, share, and spur others on to joy. Make this a week of joy by being more aware of others, cutting down on social media, and stepping out of your comfort zone. Make it your "Joy to the World" week.

> "True joy comes when you inspire, encourage, and guide someone else on a path that benefits him or her."

39

FUNDAMENTALS

I am going to start this Impact Resolution with a name-drop. I apologize for this, but as Oprah once told me . . . just kidding. Here is my name-drop: I spoke for 3M, and afterward they had a golf event. The pro in my group was none other than the legendary Hall of Famer Lee Trevino. As a golfer, this was nirvana.

We enjoyed the round of golf and talked about the fundamentals of the sport. He said golf is a simple game that people try to make too complex. Lee said, look at all the PGA golfers today; their swings are almost all the same. They all hire coaches, which Lee does not necessarily think is the secret to success. He said pro golfers pay money to coaches to help them win the US Open when the coach hasn't even won the screen door open! His theory was that fundamentals work for everyone differently.

Lee said, in golf, you just have to hit the ball in the middle of the clubhead at the right speed, consistently. It doesn't make a lot of difference on how you get the club to the ball. He compared it to your walk. He asked, How can someone fundamentally change the way you walk? It's nearly impossible to change your gait, so you need to work with what comes naturally to you.

Fundamentals are important in pretty much every aspect of life. We always think about them in sports, music, or other activities, but fundamentals are also important in your personal and professional lives. When fundamentals become a habit, you have built a structure that will stand the test of time.

Karissa Thacker is the president of Strategic Performance Solutions, and she wrote an article called "4 Fundamental Habits of Authentic Leaders" for the March 2, 2016, issue of *Fast Company* magazine. I believe these fundamentals are also true in your personal life. Karissa wrote that great leaders have four fundamental habits: One, they admit what they don't know. You cannot always be the smartest person in the room on every topic, and you can't be afraid to admit "I don't know." Secondly, they are aware of themselves and what situations make them the most difficult to work with. I call this your trigger point. You are having a great day when something or someone changes your perspective, and you go from a good mood to a bad mood in seconds. When you recognize a weakness like that, you can develop a strategy to handle the situation better. I call it your default position.

When I interview an athlete and it's not going very well, I have a question I pull out that I know will give me time to regroup. I ask them to describe themselves as an athlete, and they will talk for at least thirty seconds. Develop your very own default position and use it when you need it most. The third fundamental habit of great leaders, according to Karissa Thacker, is to have strong values and to live them. When you align your actions with your values, you can make an impact. And finally, Karissa says to make sure you listen closely to people who disagree with you. It's not easy, it's not natural, but it's part of being authentic and invaluable to your self-improvement.

IMPACT RESOLUTION

Fundamentals sometimes seem boring, but without them, you will lack consistency. This week, figure out ways you can work with your natural abilities and improve your fundamentals. Like Lee Trevino said, as long as the clubhead hits the ball in the middle, you will be fine.

40

ANTICIPATION

When a customer complains, it's already too late. You or your team were not able to anticipate the problem before it became a problem . . . and that is a problem! Proactive people have mastered the art of anticipation. They are prepared for the good, the bad, the ugly, and everything in between. Because of this mindset, even when something occurs that nobody could have possibly anticipated, they are nimble and can react better because of their preplanning.

The number-one habit listed in one of the best self-help books ever written, *The 7 Habits of Highly Effective People* by Steven Covey, is being proactive. Dr.

Covey said, "I am not a product of my circumstances. I am a product of my decisions." It's another way of saying, "No excuses."

As a sports journalist, it's always surprising to me to see how some athletes will last ten to fifteen years playing professional sports at the highest level while other athletes with just as much talent flame out sooner. I have become convinced that the athletes who stick around learn how to be proactive. They start taking the extra steps it takes to survive the cutthroat world of pro sports. These athletes anticipate the needs of their bodies and their minds. They hire personal trainers, dieticians, sports psychologists, massage therapists, chefs, and on and on. Most of us can't afford to hire a team to take care of us. However, what are you proactively doing in your "off-season" to get better in your career or life as a mom or dad?

When a customer complains, it's already too late.

In the business world, companies that reward forward thinking tend to be more prosperous. People who anticipate well are problem solvers, not problem thinkers. Pat Fallon ran one of the most successful advertising agencies in the country. His agency had clients like the *Wall Street Journal*, *Rolling Stone*, Porsche, and BMW. By the way, Fallon was not based out of Madison Avenue in New York but, rather, Minneapolis, Minnesota.

To compete against the big guns in Manhattan, Pat knew he had to create a culture where his staff would feel safe to be both creative and productive. He focused on the philosophy that the biggest risk to any business was conventional thinking. He rewarded the risk-takers, and the bottom line was proof of his success.

IMPACT
RESOLUTION

Are you playing it too safe or are you pushing yourself to anticipate risks and try new things? This week, talk it over with a friend how you can be more proactive as a parent, as a grandparent, or in your personal life.

41

POSITIVITY

I can guarantee you that the person who lights up the room when he or she enters is a person who always exudes positivity. They don't need a kite, key, and electrical storm like Ben Franklin did to light up the room; it's their positive energy that makes them glow!

From the time we are five years old, we are told that we need to have a good attitude. For some reason, we need to be reminded of it as adults too. Positive people give people energy without losing any of their own, and negative people could suck the energy out of an entire power plant.

Leaders need to model the behavior they expect from others. Captain D. Michael Abrashoff wrote an excellent book on leadership titled *It's Your Ship: Management Techniques from the Best Damn Ship in the Navy.* He writes about taking the worst ship in the Navy fleet and turning it into the best. He describes one of his central beliefs: "I'm absolutely convinced that positive, personal reinforcement is the essence of effective leadership." Aye, aye, Captain! The more successful companies I deal with, the more I believe in what Captain Abrashoff said. Positivity is contagious and can change the culture of a group or organization.

I believe the best way to spread positivity is through the power of a smile. When you are talking to someone on the phone, you can tell if they are smiling. I had the pleasure of covering Hall of Fame baseball player Kirby Puckett. Puck was almost as famous for his smile as he was for his great skills on the baseball field. You could not help but feel joy when Puck was around. This is his legacy.

We all have moments of negativity, of course. We sometimes throw ourselves a personal pity party. The world is just not fair, after all. When you have a case of the blues, how do you get yourself out of it? Author Chuck Swindoll wrote one of the most famous poems that dealt with positivity called "Attitude." Look it up if you haven't read it. In the poem, he says the longer he lives, the more convinced he is that "Life is 10 percent what happens to me and 90 percent how I react to it."

I am recovering from major back surgery as I write this book. I could not control the timing of the operation and lost some work time and business opportunities, since rehab is predicted to take at least a month. I was able to move a couple of speeches and seminars but had to give up a couple of incredible opportunities.

My friend and colleague Chris Heeter took one of the presentations I could not make. I mentioned to her that I was bummed to lose these fun events. Leave it to a positive thought leader to set me straight. She said, "Joe, you are looking at it the wrong way. Be happy that you are fortunate enough to have business that you had to give up." Positivity is a matter of perspective, and I thank Chris for having me look at my situation from a different angle. It put me in a positive frame of mind for my strenuous rehabilitation.

I have another confession to make. I am writing this particular chapter while I am watching a PGA golf tournament on TV. I love golf and won't be able to play for an entire year because of my long recovery. As I look for the silver lining, I see that I am going to save myself hundreds of dollars on green fees and lost golf balls! As I watch this tourney, I am reminded of a powerful story. Bruce Edwards was the longtime caddy for the legendary Tom Watson. He left Tom Watson for a few years to work for Greg Norman but later went back to caddy for Watson. Sadly, he died of ALS at the young age of forty-nine.

Bruce Edwards was asked one time about the difference between caddying for Greg Norman and Tom Watson. They were both amazing golfers, of course. He said that when Norman had a ball that landed in a divot, he would complain about his bad luck and mutter negative thoughts to his caddy and others. When Watson hit a ball in a divot, he would analyze the shot, grab a club, smirk at his caddy and say, "Watch this." Tom Watson won eight majors. Greg Norman won two majors and had a few famous meltdowns along the way.

IMPACT
RESOLUTION

How do you stay positive when everything and everybody around you seems to be negative? How do you respond when your life lands in a divot? Commit to figuring out some strategies that work well for you. If you have a habit of grumbling or blaming others, cut it out. A great way to move the attention away from yourself is to see if you can be a mood changer for a few people by winning them over with your smile and positivity.

42

COMMUNICATION

The number-one reason that marriages fail is a lack of communication. The number-one reason that friendships fail is lack of communication. The number-one reason that businesses fail is lack of communication. Are you starting to see a pattern here?

How you communicate has a direct impact on how productive you are, how happy you feel, and how significant your impact is. One of the biggest obstacles to effective communication is distraction. You can't actually converse with someone while you are looking at your phone or your computer. You need to focus and be all-in. Have you ever been at a party or an event when you are talking to someone and you can tell that they are looking around for someone more important to talk to? You think it must mean that you are boring to them, but actually they are the ones who are weak at communication and, quite frankly, rude.

> *How you communicate has a direct impact on how productive you are, how happy you feel, and how significant your impact is.*

Anna Liotta is an expert on generational dynamics and travels the world speaking on the topic. She has not only studied it for the past twenty-five years but has also lived it. Anna is the youngest of nineteen children. (That is not a typo.) That's six generations in her immediate family when they sit down at the table for Thanksgiving. The table must take up half the house!

There are now seven or eight generations in the workplace, and let's face it, the baby boomers don't always communicate well with the Gen Xers and the millennials. Anna's research shows that the best way to communicate with someone from a different generation is to communicate the way they prefer. For example, if they send you a text, do not pick up the phone and call them. They just let you know that texting is their preferred method of communication.

Most parents have had an experience where they call their son or daughter on the phone and get no answer. They follow that up with a text and get an answer back within seconds. That is what Anna is talking about.

One of the most important aspects of communicating via email or text is tone. Sometimes it's very hard to detect the tone of a message. For example, a joke might be misunderstood and can get lost in translation. I admit that I am a fan of sarcasm, but as a friend once told me, be careful because there is always a shred of truth in sarcasm.

Punctuation can also cause big issues and hilarious results. For example, there is a big difference in these two sentences: Let's eat Grandpa. Let's eat, Grandpa. A comma has never made good old gramps happier.

IMPACT
RESOLUTION

Talking is still the number-one and best form of communication, so make sure you listen more than you talk. If you are thinking of what you are going to say next, you are not listening. So here is your goal this week: leave every conversation with the other person feeling better about themselves. It could be what you say, or it could be what you choose not to say, but one thing is for sure: you have the opportunity to make an impact with your communication.

43

E = ENERGY, ENTHUSIASM, ENGAGEMENT

This week's Impact Resolution is a bundle of E's. None of them can be done with ease, and they are much more powerful together. Energy, enthusiasm, and engagement are far more effective, with E for effort. People who manage the E's tend to drive in the left lane in life. They get more done in one day than some people can get done in one week. People with energy can have a contagious impact on a group. Experts now say that instead of time management, people should think of it in terms of energy management.

I had a revelation about energy management and focus while recovering from major back surgery. In the month I took off work to recover, I planned to read, work on my business plan, and binge-watch a few shows on Netflix that I never seem to have time to view. My plan lasted exactly one day. Instead, I decided that I should write this book.

After being my all-star nurse for one week, my wonderful wife went back to work. I began writing that morning at eight and was so wrapped up in my work that when Laura called to check on me, I was shocked to learn it was two o'clock. I had nothing on my calendar, no meetings scheduled, no calls to make, and no emails to return. Distractions hurt progress, and I had none.

> *Leaders who show energy and enthusiasm tend to engage with their employees, customers, and friends.*

The nineteenth-century American philosopher and poet Ralph Waldo Emerson has a famous quote that still rings true today: "Nothing great was ever achieved without enthusiasm." Some people question the importance of enthusiasm. They say it is a trait natural to extroverts. My experience has really shown otherwise. Introverts come by enthusiasm naturally as well. Leaders who show energy and enthusiasm tend to engage with their employees, customers, and friends. A lack of enthusiasm brings a lack of engagement. Unlike Larry David in the television series *Curb Your Enthusiasm*, if you use positive energy when you face life's challenges, you have a better chance to thrive and survive.

Amplifon, a worldwide distributor of Miracle-Ear hearing aids and other products and services in this space, is very involved in the communities they serve. Recently, the company was raising money for a children's hospital, and some of the executives at the corporate office got especially creative. President and CEO Marc Lundeberg announced he would dress up as Lady Gaga and serve cake in the lunchroom if the fundraising goals were met. Just a few days later, Marc put on his "Poker Face," dressed up like he was "Born This Way," and made a somewhat realistic-looking Gaga! It was a risk and out of the norm for sure, but Mark engaged his team and helped raise money for a worthy charity.

IMPACT
RESOLUTION

This week, try to make your energy and enthusiasm so noticeable that they are contagious. See if it helps you feel more engaged with others. Also, when you see someone who is a force of nature when it comes to the E's, sit back and watch the magic. Study how it works.

44

FEARLESSNESS

Sam was in a hurry to get to the airport in Las Vegas. He had just given the keynote speech at a national conference, and after talking to some of the folks at his book table, he realized he was running late. A woman who was at his presentation noticed that Sam was waiting for a cab and offered to give him a ride to the airport. It was a ride that neither of them would ever forget.

Sam Richter is an internationally recognized expert on sales intelligence and online reputation management. He can find information online that Google only wishes they could find. Sam teaches clients all over the world, always closing his presentation with the story of how he became an expert at finding information on the internet. His first major search was a success when he found a person he had been wanting to meet for decades—his birth mother.

As nice as the lady was to give Sam a ride, she had an outside motive. You see, Rane was just nineteen years old when she found herself pregnant and choosing adoption. She was only able to hold her son for a few minutes before giving him to the adoption agency. Rane had to be both desperate and fearless to make the big ask. She took a deep breath, dug deep into her soul, and asked Sam if he would help find her son.

The very next day, Rane emailed Sam all the information she had on the birth of her son, and by the next evening, Sam sent her an email that she now describes as a miracle. Sam had not only found her son, but he also sent pictures and contact information for him!

His name was Jeremy, and he was living in Idaho with his wife and two children. A local radio station heard about Rane's story and arranged for her to fly to meet her son and give him her first hug in thirty years! We have all heard the old saying, "No guts, no glory." She was fearless enough to ask and now has the glory and a story. It isn't a Hollywood ending; it's a new beginning!

There is power in being fearless. It helps you tackle the imaginary hurdles that seem to perpetually surround us. Like Rane, it can be as simple as asking for help.

If you are afraid to ask someone you are attracted to for a date, it is not going to happen. If you don't have the guts to discuss a brewing personal problem, it will become a huge issue. If you let fear rule when it comes to asking for the sale, the sale will not be made. Be brave. Be fearless.

If you don't have the guts to discuss a brewing personal problem, it will become a huge issue.

IMPACT RESOLUTION

How can you make fearlessness a part of your DNA? Think of times you were afraid to take action, but you did anyway and were happy with the results. American film director and screenwriter Jennifer Lee said, "Be fearless in the pursuit of what sets your soul on fire." Be brave. Be fearless.

45

COMPASSION

Whenever one of our photojournalists is sent to cover a high school game where the winning team earns a trip to the state tournament, it doesn't matter what the sport is; there is going to be a big celebration. Our photographers know that we will use that priceless video in our next newscast. We call those "money shots." The thrill of victory, the pure joy of accomplishment, the hog pile on the field or gym floor—you can't beat those moments.

Two Minnesota high schools, Moundsview and Totino-Grace, faced each other in the state high school baseball tournament. Teams that qualify for the state tourney are thrilled because they get to play their games at Target Field, the home of the Minnesota Twins. It's one of the most beautiful stadiums in baseball and a great perk for the kids.

Moundsview was leading four to nothing and needed just one more out to win the section title. Ty Koehn was on the mound and threw a fastball on the outside corner of the plate for strike three. It was game over. Celebration ensued for all of Moundsview, except for one player.

While his teammates were yelling and cheering and tossing their gloves in the air, Ty Koehn ran toward home plate to hug the dejected batter he just struck out. Jack Kocon of Totino-Grace and Ty Koehn had grown up playing Little League and traveling base-ball together. Even though they went to different high schools, they remained friends. If you did not get a lump in your throat watching the video, you were not breathing. It was an amazing display of sportsmanship and compassion!

Ty felt it was only right to console his friend before celebrating with his team. You are lucky if you have a friend like that. Several days later, when Jack Kocon's parents held a graduation party for him, a lot of the players from the Moundsview team, including Ty, showed up.

Compassion makes you sensitive to another person's feelings, their pain, and their confusion. It brings you to take action.

I've seen more and more companies making compassion a part of their workplace culture. Jeff Weiner, CEO of LinkedIn, delivered a commencement address to the Wharton School of the University of Pennsylvania, which I saw on YouTube. Jeff Weiner told the students, "I can tell you with absolute conviction that managing compassion is not just a better way to build a team. It's a better way to build a company." He later explained his philosophy, saying that if you really want to lift people up, you need to see things through their lens. That's compassion.

IMPACT
RESOLUTION

Think about times people showed compassion toward you and how powerful that was for you. Discuss it with your accountability partner or friend to come up with more examples of compassion in action. The rewards of compassion are often profound.

46

PREPARATION

I like to ask business leaders what sets them apart from the competition, and I always tell them the answer cannot be "our people." Believe it or not, your competition has good people who are smart and dedicated too. There are a lot of great answers, such as innovation or integrity, but one of the best answers in today's global economy is preparation. Be prepared for anything that is thrown your way, and if it's something completely out of the blue, be prepared to be nimble enough to make changes quickly.

One of the exercises I use in my seminars is something I call the Trigger Point. Participants discuss this scenario: You are having a great day knocking things off your list when you get a call or someone comes to your office to talk. They complain, make an unreasonable request, or say something negative. Suddenly you just lose your momentum. Productivity came to a screeching halt, and you went from having a good day to having a bad day.

The first part of the exercise is to recognize what scenario sets you off. The second part of the exercise is to come up with some strategies that will help you control what you can control, which is mainly your attitude, and let go of the rest.

The key is to come up with a default position, something that will work every time you are stumped or flustered. If someone comes to complain about a colleague not pulling their own weight or a shortage of vacation time, what is your default response? Choose a comment or behavior plan that will help you remain patient. For example, you could say, "Bill, I really understand your situation and want to help you come up with a solution. I am on a deadline now, so could you come back after lunch so we can further discuss?" By the time he comes back, you have had time to cool down and are ready to lend a listening ear.

I've gotten some unique answers with the Trigger Point exercise. One person suggested starting a meeting off with a compliment on a recent project that they worked on. It can help lower the temperature in the room. Another tactic that works well is to make them part of the process. How would you suggest we solve this issue? It's a nice way of saying: *Please don't come in here with a problem unless you already have an idea for the solution.*

When we hire interns or young professionals at the station, I always tell them that everyone on board works very hard. It's the person who is better prepared and is determined to work smart who has the most success.

> It's the person who is better prepared and is determined to work smart who has the most success.

IMPACT
RESOLUTION

This week, think of ways you can be better prepared in all phases of your personal and professional life. Identify your trigger point and how you are going to handle it when somebody or something sets you off. The Boy Scouts' motto for years has been "Be prepared." It has remained their slogan because it is that important.

47

INTEGRITY

The most important asset you have is not your home or your bank account but your integrity. How do you act when you know nobody is watching? What do you do when you are at a store and they give you too much change? Do you put it in your pocket, or do you make it right? You cannot cut corners or take shortcuts when it comes to integrity. It's more than just being honest; it's a way to conduct your life and your business.

I left television for three years to become president of a media and marketing company. It was an opportunity to help grow the business and to be 100 percent transparent. I had a chance to earn equity in the company and reap some great financial rewards. I was also a little burned out from working nights, weekends, and holidays, as the TV schedule, especially in the sports world, can be demanding. In my new position, I had more freedom with my schedule and more time for my family.

The company I was in charge of was part of a much larger holding company owned by a dynamic entrepreneur who seemed to have the golden touch. He owned over thirty companies and had investments and operating control in many others. My team did media and marketing programs for many of these companies and others outside the organization. It seemed as if people lined up to invest with this genius, the goose who was laying golden eggs all over the business world.

Long story short, while 95 percent of the businesses were legit, the holding company turned out to be part of one of the largest Ponzi schemes in US history. The owner of the company and five others went to prison. Most of the companies either imploded or were sold off to pay off investors who were ripped off in the illegal scheme. It was a mess, and a lot of honest, hardworking people lost their jobs.

Like most of the employees, I had no idea what was going on. As I tell people who ask me if I knew anything, I say, "If you rob a bank, do you go around and tell a bunch of people?" There was guilt by association, and even though it was not fair, many of us had to live with it.

Obviously, the owner of this company was narcissistic and had no integrity, but when I look back, I always think of a speech I heard him give often. He was proud of the six core values that the company developed and would tell any audience that those traits were the basis of how he led and how decisions were made. One of the core values was integrity, and every time he mentioned it in his speech, he would always say, "Integrity—we are still working on that one." He would chuckle and the audience would too. Eventually we all found out that in sarcasm, there is always a shred of truth. In this case, it was destructive and totally illegal.

The closer we are with people, the higher our expectations are when it comes to integrity. That is a good thing. I have gotten rid of friends who lack integrity. It is empowering to get rid of toxic relationships.

Too many people work hard at just earning a stellar reputation. But if you work that hard on your integrity, you will not have to worry about your reputation because it will be an asset you can be proud of.

IMPACT
RESOLUTION

This week, think of people you know who have impeccable integrity. Do they have to worry about their reputations? Also, take a good look at your circle of friends and acquaintances who might be a bad influence or dragging you down in some way or another. Have the courage to either end those relationships or make yourself less available.

48

SELFLESSNESS

The easiest way to describe the meaning of selflessness: mother. I know there are a lot of amazing dads out there, but there is no question that selflessness is one of the hallmark qualities of motherhood.

I was doing a presentation for a group of lab professionals who are certified and highly specialized. At the conference, I met a bright young lady by the name of Geeta. She was from Guyana and grew up in complete poverty. Her family had to walk a mile just to retrieve clean water. Geeta was a good student, and the family saved up just enough money to get her to the US to attend York College in Queens. On a student visa in

1998, she could only work a limited number of hours, so money was very tight.

Every day, Geeta took the bus to school. The fee was $1.25, and there were many days in which she had to count her pennies to pay for the ride to school. One bus driver noticed this and asked if she was having trouble coming up with the bus fare. She sheepishly admitted that she was barely getting by and some days she would not eat much so she could get through school and eventually help her family.

The bus driver made her a deal. He told her that a dime was the same weight as a bus token. She would put a dime in the slot, and it would be their little secret. On Friday, the bus driver would give Geeta his schedule for the next week and sometimes she would go to school three hours early just to get a ride from this gentleman who cared enough and was aware enough to make a difference.

Geeta rode the bus for a year and a half, until she was able to move closer to the school in a less expensive apartment. She went back to the bus company to find the driver but found out that he had retired, and they could not give her his contact information. Geeta offered to reimburse the bus company the amount she had saved during that difficult time, but they told her not to worry about it.

I used my reporting skills and even got the investigative unit of my TV station involved in trying to find this bus driver. We think his first name was Dwayne. He was African American and wore glasses and his heart on his sleeve. His route was Q112 that ran from Ozone Park to Guy Brewer Boulevard on the York College campus. We do not know if the bus driver is alive or not, but we are pretty certain he has no idea the impact he had on Geeta, her family, and her future. Remember, Silent Impact has a snowball effect. In this case, it was generational.

Geeta is now a clinical lab scientist who is getting her master's degree in public health while she works and raises a family. Her husband is originally from Africa and was earning four dollars an hour washing dishes while he went to college in America. He is now an attorney, and they have two wonderful young sons. Geeta and her husband have been able to help their families back home financially. She says that the bus driver who helped her so many years ago is on her Mount Rushmore of Influence, and she thinks of him often. Geeta does not think she would have made it through school without that man, who had a heart bigger than the bus he drove.

When you are selfless, you expect nothing in return. If you played a sport or have kids who play sports, you know we always try to preach that an assist is just as good as scoring, whether it be a goal or a basket. In hockey, they called Wayne Gretzky "The Great One." Nobody in the history of the National Hockey League scored more goals. He put the puck in the net 894 times, 93 more than the legendary Gordie Howe. But what made Gretzky earn his nickname was that he was a total team player. He had more assists than any player in NHL history. He had 1,963 assists in regular season play, which is more than twice his goal total and over 700 more assists than any other player who laced up the skates.

Wayne Gretzky and the 1990s driver of Route Q112 in Queens have three things in common. They were both selfless, made a big and lasting impact, and can be considered great ones!

IMPACT
RESOLUTION

This week, think of ways you can be selfless. Look around at the people you know and think about which ones have mastered the art of selflessness. Remember, it's the little things that sometimes turn out to be the important things.

49

OPEN MINDEDNESS

Sometimes we close our minds without even realizing it. We are so sure of ourselves that we are not open to new ideas or new ways to solve problems. Answer this: "What color is a yield sign?"

If you answered yellow, you are like 90 percent of the people. The truth is that yield signs have been red since the early 1970s. Open-minded people do not care if they are right, they care if they understand and like to learn new things.

Try this simple exercise: Close your fist tight and hold it in front of you. Try to use it to catch an imaginary ball. That's not going to work. Now open your hand out wide. Easy to catch a ball now, and even easier if your eyes are open. Your mind is like your hand. If it's closed, it's hard to function, and you most certainly can't catch anything!

Early in my broadcast career, I was the sports anchor at WBAY-TV in Green Bay, Wisconsin. In Titletown USA, we covered the Packers (pretty much) 365 days a year. The great outdoors was also something that we focused on quite a bit because the folks in northeastern Wisconsin absolutely love to hunt and fish.

My partner in the sports department was a guy by the name of Bill Jartz. He was a big, friendly, charismatic guy who made my job an absolute joy. Bill told me he wanted to do a story on a guy who wrote a cookbook with a bunch of recipes for venison. Since deer hunting season had just started, it made some sense, but I was against it. I said, "Bill, we have a sportscast to put on the air. Why would we turn our segment into something Martha Stewart would do?" It just didn't fit our brand.

Bill insisted. I told him to go ahead with his story idea, even though I was pretty sure that a segment with a guy in blaze orange who thought he was the Betty Crocker of venison would be a flop.

To this day, there has not been a story in over thirty years of TV that got more of a reaction! Boy, am I glad I did not let my close-mindedness get in the way. Our station received calls for weeks with people wanting information on how to get the venison cookbook. The receptionist at WBAY-TV actually got mad at us because she felt she was spending half her day selling cookbooks. The author spent so much time filling orders for the book that he hardly got to deer hunt that season. I have the feeling he made enough money that he was eating lobster and filet mignon all winter instead of preparing recipes out of his cookbook.

We can all work to suspend judgment and keep an open mind about why someone might be struggling.

We've done some internal research on companies and organizations of various sizes, looking at difficult employees specifically. We usually found that they were unhappy because the job was too big for them. They needed help, they were frustrated, and their colleagues were very frustrated. Sometimes that person was going through a difficult life circumstance, like a sick parent or a marriage issue. We can all work to suspend judgment and keep an open mind about why someone might be struggling. Perhaps your flailing colleague really does need to be ushered into a different role or an entirely different company, but in the meantime, try to imagine their life circumstances and how you could make a lasting impact.

IMPACT RESOLUTION

Think of ways you can be more open-minded and less judgmental. If someone who dwells in the negative has your ear, take practical steps to limit exposure. Decide for yourself to suspend judgment and see the situation through a different lens. When you can look at an issue or a person from a different angle, you will often make a breakthrough. When this happens, make sure you take time to pat yourself on the back!

50

CARING

There are two types of people you will meet in this world. It's easy to tell the difference because they operate with two different motives. The first group thinks, "Hi, nice to meet you. How can you serve me?" The second group thinks, "Hi, nice to meet you. How can I serve you?" How refreshing to feel like someone cares about you, and even better when both people have the same attitude!

People who volunteer care. People who share their time, talents, resources, and knowledge without looking for anything in return care. I have yet to meet anyone who gives of themselves and is miserable. People who care make an impact.

In our research, my team found out that employees want three things from the company they work for.

1. They want to work for a successful organization that is going to be around for a while.

2. They want a chance to grow along with the company. They want opportunities for career advancement.

3. They want to work for a company that cares. They want a company that not only cares about their employees, but also one that cares about the communities they serve.

Did you know people aren't leaving their jobs because they feel underpaid? They are leaving their jobs because they feel underappreciated. Caring is more than just saying you care. Caring is marked by action. When my good friend Mike McKinley lost his wife to cancer, his friend and colleague Lou Heckler called him every single day for a year. Sometimes it was to let Mike grieve, sometimes it was to tell a joke, sometimes it was to check in, but every single time, it was to let Mike know that he cared. That action of caring had a tremendous impact on Mike. By the way, while recovering from back surgery, I've gotten a call or text from Mike every day. Caring is contagious!

I covered a high school hockey player from Edina, Minnesota, named Ben Peyton, who was paralyzed after getting hit in a game. For a few days, the doctors were not sure that Ben would survive. Thankfully, he did, and while he has some physical limitations today, he has a career, many friends, and lives a quality life.

You can only imagine the pain and heartbreak his parents, John and Nancy, were going through during this incredibly challenging time. The family agreed to let me document Ben's journey through a series of television stories. There were many emotional moments of courage and love, but one moment in particular stood out to me. John was so overwhelmed by the outpouring of support and care that came from their community and across the nation. As difficult as it was for them to go through the pain and disappointment of Ben's injury, it was remarkable to experience how many people truly cared.

IMPACT
RESOLUTION

This week, and every week for that matter, we can all do a better job of letting people know we care. A quick phone call, a text, or a surprise gift can let someone know you care about their circumstances. The next time you are in a store and see something you know someone would love, if it's in your budget, buy it. Be generous with your words, to friends and strangers alike. It doesn't cost anything and can change some-one's day.

51

CHANGE

Most people feel uncomfortable when they leave their area code. Why is change so hard? We have two choices when it comes to change: embrace it or fight it. Either response can be contagious in a professional environment. When you battle change, you are fighting for a losing cause.

Once upon a time, there were people who made a good living selling facsimile machines. If you've never faxed anything, then you are younger than me. One of my early speeches was to a group of video-store owners. Many of them were scared because they saw the future coming. Some of them started to work on their plan B. They had a storefront in a good location, loyal employees, and customers with whom they had built relationships. They were not only able to embrace change, but they were able to survive because they were nimble and did not let fear paralyze them.

When there is change in a corporate situation, it's more important than ever for leaders to be clear, concise, and get buy-in from key constituents. One of my clients, a worldwide Fortune 500 company, was moving their corporate offices from a suburban setting in a major metropolitan area to a high-rise office building right in the heart of downtown. It was something the company needed to do to improve their profile and to continue growing in an increasingly competitive marketplace.

As you might expect, some employees did not like the change. Most of it had to do with dealing with the unknown and the unfamiliar. The commute would be longer, parking would cost money, and more than anything, they liked their current office. The company leaders knew of this going into the change. Long before the actual physical move took place, they developed strategies to help employees adjust. They took small groups on tours of the new facility and pointed out the new and improved lunchroom, workout facility, and day-care options. They even arranged tours of the surrounding area, so employees would be familiar with the area restaurants, bars, stores, and coffee shops. By the time they were ready for the move, most of the employees had embraced the change.

Truth be told, life would be pretty boring without change. If you are willing to step out of your comfort zone, you will find that opening your mind to change means you are growing and learning. Ask any pro fisherman about where to catch fish, and they will tell you it depends. The conditions are changing all the time and the anglers who adapt to change are the most successful.

> *Truth be told, life would be pretty boring without change.*

IMPACT
RESOLUTION

This week, think about some of the major changes in your personal and professional life and how you handled them. Part of growth is owning up to moments we would like to have done differently. When you handle it like a pro, be proud. Sometimes success means cutting your losses and going in a new direction. Sometimes success means staying the course, even when things feel tough. That's why it's so valuable to assess your experiences and learn from them. It will make you more adaptable. Change can change things for the better!

52

LOVE

There has been no greater theme for songwriting than the complicated subject of love. "All You Need is Love" was written in 1967 by John Lennon and sung by the Beatles. It has stood the test of time. The message is still relevant today with so many people suffering from mental health issues, bullying, relationship troubles, and overwhelming pressures to succeed.

Most of the time when we think about love, we think about loving other people, but we can love anything from nature to reading books to our jobs. The reality is that when you love someone or something, it increases your happiness. Love is a risk because you are putting your heart on the line. That is why there are so many songs written about heartache and broken love. Just remember the famous words of Alfred Lord Tennyson, who wrote, "Tis better to have loved and lost than never to have loved at all." (Full disclosure here folks, I had to google this one.)

You can always tell when you run into someone who loves their job. Their energy is contagious. It's positive. It's powerful. Can you think of anyone who loves their job that isn't also very good at it? Probably not. Unfortunately, too many people are just putting in the hours to earn a paycheck. They are miserable but don't know what to do about it.

Can you think of anyone who loves their job that isn't also very good at it? Probably not.

When my mother passed away in 2014, I gave the eulogy. It was an honor but a challenging task. I wanted to make sure to capture the essence of my mother for those who attended. The first thing I did was ask my five siblings to independently come up with one word to describe the woman who brought them into this world. It was a terrific exercise because we all came up with different traits. It helped me paint a picture of her life and legacy. During my preparation, I felt I needed something else to tie the entire eulogy together.

That's when Paul, George, John, and Ringo of the Beatles came to the rescue. I was listening to the radio in my car when the song "The End" came on. It's the last song in a three-song medley on their *Abbey Road* album. The song ends with this line: "And in the end, the love you take is equal to the love you make." This was perfect! It described my mom's life perfectly. She created a lot of love and got a lot of love in return.

IMPACT
RESOLUTION

Your legacy is everyone you touch, everyone you have an impact on during your whole life. Consider this week your own personal Beatlemania. All you need is love! All you need to do is work daily to create it and enjoy the love you get in return.

ACKNOWLEDGMENTS

There's a great scene in the movie *The Blues Brothers* where John Belushi and Dan Aykroyd's characters go around the country to "get the band back together." When I started writing this book, I knew I had to tap my inner Jake and Elwood Blues because I needed to get the *Silent Impact* band back together again. My first call was to Heidi Sheard. She is not only my editor, but she is a trusted advisor and has the ability to keep me on track. I would not have written the book without her in the band. I wanted Jay Monroe to design the interior and exterior of the book since he did such a stellar job on my first book. He's given both books personality and soul. In honor of Jake and Elwood, I will call him our "Soul Man." I also knew that I wanted my book published by Amy Quale and her trusted team at Wise Ink Creative Publishing. All you need to know is that

I have sent many aspiring authors to Wise Ink for their expertise.

I would like to sincerely thank the people who let me tell their stories of impact. They are collectively providing this blueprint by which we can all be inspired! I do believe there is so much more good going on in this world than bad and we need to focus on the good, and in turn, we will inspire others. I also want to thank the companies and organizations I have worked with since *Silent Impact* was first published in 2014. What I learned from great leaders and amazing people across a diverse group of companies, associations and sports teams is the basis for this book.

I am a very lucky guy. I love sports and television, and get to work in that setting with talented colleagues at KSTP-TV every day! I'm so grateful they also allow me to follow my passion of learning about the power of impact and speaking about it around the country.

I have immense gratitude for my family. They inspire me every day. My wife, Laura, is a giver, has a heart of gold, and has made me a better person. She is also the main reason we have three amazing kids, Natalie, Gaby, and Matthew. I am fortunate to say I not only love my kids, but I really like them too! Our love has grown since our daughter, Natalie, married Dustin, and we've welcomed an incredible granddaughter named Remy.

AUTHOR NOTE

I will be the first to admit that I am not an expert on the 52 Impact Resolutions in this book. I have researched and continue to study why and how people make an impact on their friends, colleagues, children, and even complete strangers. Every single one of these traits can help you become more aware and intentional with the impact you are making on this world. I am a reporter at heart, so I love to do the research. As a reporter, I believe in the power of the story and believe I can make an impact through telling these stories. I did everything possible to make sure I attributed every quote I used in this book to the rightful owner. Some of the information is fairly universal, and some of the suggestions are based on some common ideas and information. In other words, it was with great effort that I did everything I could not to borrow or steal any intellectual information from anyone. If I did by accident, I apologize. You can call my wife, she is a lawyer. (She is a divorce lawyer, and if you sue me, I might need one myself!)

ABOUT THE AUTHOR

Joe Schmit is an award-winning broadcaster, community leader, author, and popular keynote speaker, and was recently honored with the Next Level award by the Minnesota chapter of the National Speakers Association. His book, *Silent Impact: Influence Through Purpose, Persistence & Passion* is now in its second edition and has won numerous awards. As a sports broadcaster, Joe has covered every major sporting event in the past three decades and has interviewed many of the biggest names in sports. He joined KSTP-TV in 1985 and has won eighteen Emmys from the National Television Academy. He was also honored with a National Head-liner Award in 2001.

Before joining KSTP-TV in 1985, Joe was Sports Director for WBAY-TV in Green Bay, Wisconsin. His career also included positions as weekend sports anchor for KCRG-TV in Cedar Rapids, Iowa, and WKBT-TV in La Crosse, Wisconsin. Joe earned his degree in Mass Communications from the University of Wisconsin-La Crosse.

Joe left broadcasting for three years to become President of PMMG, a media and marketing company that had clients such as Polaroid, Sun Country Airlines, Ubid, Fingerhut, and others. He was also the spokes-person for Sun Country Airlines and appeared on all their TV and radio commercials.

Joe is a long-time youth mentor, committed to advocating for a number of community organizations, with Big Brothers and Big Sisters at the top of his list. He is a past president and board member of Big Brothers and Big Sisters of the Greater Twin Cities. He helped raise over $3 million for the organization through the Joe Schmit Celebrity Golf Tournament which had a sixteen-year run. In 2000, he was the winner of the Jim Kelly Distinguished Service Award from Big Brothers and Big Sisters and in 2001, a winner of the Odyssey Award for commitment to youth mentorship. Joe was also honored as the Juvenile Diabetes Research Fund (JDRF) Community Leader of the Year in 2005. He is past president and board member of the Fairway Foundation and has contributed time to many other charitable organizations. Joe and his wife, Laura, chaired a $4 million capital campaign for VEAP, the largest food shelf in Minnesota.

"We make our biggest impressions when we aren't trying to be impressive."

–JOE SCHMIT, SPEAKER AND AWARD-WINNING BROADCASTER

EPIC IMPACT PROGRAMS
HALF DAY SEMINARS
INTERACTIVE KEYNOTES
BREAKOUT SESSIONS

 BOOK JOE SCHMIT
TO SPEAK AT YOUR NEXT EVENT

Joe Schmit has studied leaders who make an impact, and his message will be sure to make a positive impact at your next event! His engaging, authentic, and humorous style is wrapped around powerful stories and content that will empower every person to make deeper connections to maximize their impact on others. Joe prides himself on customizing presentations for each audience and strives to make the meeting planner look like a hero.

ACTIONABLE TAKEAWAYS

- Discover how to improve your ROI—Return on Impact Improve your team's culture with Impact Resolutions Identify and emulate your Mt. Rushmore of Influence

- Learn the secret to being an "Impact Player"

- Become a leader of impact in business and life

HAPPY CLIENTS

I simply cannot count the number of clients that have shared both in person and in writing how much they enjoyed Joe's session. The impact made by this group of phenomenal leaders, both professionally and personally, is impressive! Fantastic job!

—DeAnna Busby-Rast, Chief Business Development Officer, DCM Services National Conference

Thank you so much, Joe, for being you and making an IMPACT within our GCS walls. I have changed the way I do business because of you.

—Charlie Lawson President/CEO GCS

Joe's video program is a wonderful tool to help the attendees meet the challenge of carrying the conference lessons back to their teams and our over one thousand employees.

—Jack Sipes Partner and Senior Vice President, Property Management at Dominium

INTERACTIVE KEYNOTES • HALF-DAY SEMINARS • BREAKOUT SESSIONS • EPIC IMPACT YEAR-LONG PROGRAM • VIDEO SERIES

To get on Joe's calendar, call **(612) 210-8463** or email Joe at **joe@joeschmit.com**.